Proven Strategies for Successful Test Taking

Thomas M. Sherman

*Virginia Polytechnic Institute
and State University*

Terry M. Wildman

*Virginia Polytechnic Institute
and State University*

Charles E. Merrill Publishing
A Bell & Howell Company
Columbus   Toronto   London   Sydney

Published by
Charles E. Merrill Publishing Co.
A Bell & Howell Company
Columbus, Ohio 43216

This book was set in Times Roman and Helvetica.
Cover Design Coordination: Will Chenoweth.
Text Designer: Sharon Thomason
Production Coordination: Lucinda Ann Peck.

Cover Photo: Stephen J. Walsh, Associate Professor of Geography and
Director of the Center for the Application of Remote Sensing (CARS) at
Oklahoma State University. Dr. Walsh created the design from LANDSAT
data using the computer equipment available at CARS.

Library of Congress Catalog Card Number: 81–84661
International Standard Book Number: 0–675–09843–2
Printed in the United States of America
2   3   4   5   6   7   8   9   10—86   85   84   83   82

To
Janice and Bill
Jane and Justin

Contents

3

4

5

6

7

Preface

We are amazed at how little students know about taking tests. All the students in our university classes have from twelve to fourteen years of experience taking academic tests. Yet, most appear to know little about how to prepare for and take different kinds of tests; many students even study in inappropriate and counterproductive ways.

Students who are training to be teachers take courses covering how to construct good tests. During these classes, we include discussions of how students may take advantage of test characteristics. Most students express surprise when we describe how to increase scores on multiple-choice or essay exams. Students have reported to us that they have used these ideas later to improve test scores and grades in other courses. We believe that every student could profit from knowing how to take tests effectively. That is the purpose of this book: to describe in a simple, direct way how to become a good test taker.

Whether you are a student in a university or a four-year, community, or junior college, the principles or actions described in this book should help you make good grades. We have included information covering three aspects of test taking: knowing the purpose and characteristics of different kinds of tests, knowing how to take tests, and knowing how to prepare for tests. In addition, we have included some advice about working with your teachers and preparing for exams that should be helpful in getting better tests scores.

There are many books available on how to study and several on how to take tests. This book is different from these others in an important way. We show you how to benefit directly from your study by describing how to take tests well. It is really not enough to know what was taught in a course. It is also not enough to know how to take tests. The two must be combined into a plan to attack and master tests. In other words, you must be able to demonstrate on a test what you have learned during a course. We will suggest many study techniques, but not in a general way. We will show you how to study specifically for tests of various kinds so that you can learn, remember, and use your learning to achieve good grades.

Read, learn, and use the principles in this book. If you do, you will have a better understanding of the purposes and characteristics of tests, and this understanding will certainly lead to an increased ability to perform well on tests.

We are grateful to several individuals for their assistance in preparing this book. Hilda Borko, Ailene Wartenberg, and Betty Mahan provided much helpful advice. To Terry Stevers, Dottie Wasta, and Susan Blanton, we owe thanks for their careful typing and proofreading. We also thank the following reviewers for the comments that helped shape our final manuscript: Teresa Deen, Kennesaw College; Dolores Enderle, Siena Heights College; Bruce Sturm, De Anza College; and Elaine Cherney, Michigan State University.

Principles

2

3

4

5

6

True-False, Matching, and Short-Answer Tests   **95**

7

Maximizing Your Test Scores   **119**

Becoming an
Aggressive Test Taker

You have probably received a score lower than you deserved on many tests. In fact, many students' test scores reflect less knowledge than they actually have. Almost every one of us has had the uncomfortable feeling after a test that, even though we knew the material covered, we did not do well. Or even worse, we may have believed we did very well on a test, only to get a lower grade than expected. Sometimes these feelings of frustration are made worse when we find that a fellow student, who did not seem to know the material as well as we did, received a higher grade.

Unfortunately, many students seem to believe there is nothing they can do to improve their test scores, and they give up ever being recognized as excellent students. It is easy to understand why students feel like giving up. Why bother with hard work when it does not pay off?

MAKING YOUR EFFORTS PAY OFF

In this book, we want to help you see how to make your efforts pay off. Anyone can significantly improve test scores by learning the characteristics of tests, knowing the purpose for taking tests, and understanding how to prepare for tests. In other words, you must learn *how* to take tests. To some readers it may sound foolish for us to say you need to learn how to take tests. After all, you have been taking tests for at least ten to twelve years. However, learning to take tests can be a lot like learning to drive a car. You can learn to drive on your own, but given no instruction, explanation, or opportunity to watch anyone drive, it probably would take a long time to learn to drive safely. Test taking, like driving a car, is a very complex activity, requiring practice and skill. The majority of students, because they receive no help in learning how to take tests, develop bad habits that reduce their ability to get good test scores. Other students never recognize positive actions they can take to improve test scores. The skilled test taker, like the skilled driver, is alert, recognizes problems, and responds to them in an effective way; whereas the unskilled person is unprepared for surprises and may panic. When you are being tested, your success depends not only upon how much you know, but upon how well you *use* your knowledge of the material covered on the test.

LEARNING TO BE AGGRESSIVE

The purpose of the information in this book is to help you make yourself into a skilled test taker. Throughout this book, we will refer to skilled test takers as *aggressive test takers*. Many students approach tests passively by only reading and rereading assigned material and class notes. Their approach is essentially passive because there is no intentional activity directed at specifically preparing for performing well on a test.

An aggressive and skilled driver always drives with the future in mind, carefully watches the road ahead and behind for obstacles or signs of danger, prepares for special road conditions, makes certain the vehicle is in good condition, anticipates possible problems, and acts positively to avoid danger. A passive automobile driver waits for dangerous situations to happen and *then* reacts. Skilled drivers are not lucky, they are smart. The same is true of skilled test takers: they are not lucky, they are smart and aggressive in the way they attack tests by preparing for the test and knowing how to take the test.

You can prepare yourself to attack tests aggressively and with confidence. As an aggressive test taker, you will know that it is your action, not luck, that determines whether you will do well on a test. As an aggressive test taker, you will understand the purposes for which tests are given. You will understand how to take tests to increase your scores. And, you will know how to specifically prepare for different kinds of tests. In short, you can make yourself an aggressive test taker and know how to effectively use the knowledge you possess to get the best possible test score.

The key to becoming an aggressive test taker is to learn and use the information in this book. We have tried to make the task easy for you by describing the actions of an aggressive test taker in terms of *action principles*. We have divided these action principles into three types: actions to help you *understand* tests, actions to help you *prepare* for tests, and actions to help you *attack* tests. We will describe how you can use these action principles with six different kinds of commonly used tests: multiple choice, essay, open book, matching, true-false, and short answer. We have also included some additional action principles on studying for tests and maximizing test scores. These action principles will help you become an aggressive test taker if you make them a regular part of your test taking. Before presenting these action principles, we will discuss the following basic characteristics of tests.

- Tests *sample* your knowledge.
- Tests are measuring devices.
- Teachers' motives for giving tests vary.

TESTS SAMPLE YOUR KNOWLEDGE

Any test is basically an attempt to sample what you know. The term *sample* means that tests are designed to measure only a portion of what you know. From this sample of your knowledge, the instructor determines how much you have learned. Only rarely, if ever, will you encounter a teacher who tries to test you on everything you know. The problem facing the instructor is very similar to the one faced by the Gallup organization when it attempts to measure public opinion. For example, to predict the winner of an election, pollsters will select a small number of people (a sample) and ask these people for whom they will vote. From the responses of this small group, the Gallup organization will make a prediction about how the entire population will vote. The key problem in making such predictions is to identify people who are similar to the larger group who will vote. If the sample is representative of the entire population, then the prediction will be accurate. On the other hand, if the sample does not accurately represent the larger group, the prediction will be inaccurate.

Since teachers only *sample* what you know, your total knowledge must be demonstrated through your answers to questions that cover only a small portion of what you have learned. You *and* the instructor face a difficult task here. You can imagine an instructor's problems in designing a 50-minute test to assess what you have learned over many weeks. Think of some of the decisions the instructor must make about content and format:

- Of the hundreds of bits of information available, which ones should I include on this test?
- What should I have students do with this information?
- Should I ask students to recall information verbatim?
- Should I require students to recall information in their own words?
- Should I require students to construct responses?
- Is it reasonable to expect students to use facts and rules differently from the way they were covered in class?
- What kind of test should I construct? An objective test (multiple choice, for example) allows me to ask a greater number of questions.

On the other hand, an essay test may allow me to pursue a point in greater depth.

As the student, you have your own questions:

- What content will be covered?
- What will I be expected to do?
- How will the test be presented?

As students and as instructors, we have seen both sides of the problem. We know as well as you do that instructors sometimes make unfair and unwise decisions about what to include on tests. In the worst of cases, a test will not represent at all what has been taught and studied by students. In these cases, the students must play an extremely anxiety-provoking guessing game. In most cases, however, the instructor will do a good sampling job and will give ample information about the kind of test you will be given. A poor test score most often is the result of not preparing for what we should have known was coming. Because tests sample knowledge, you must either know everything covered, or you must accurately predict what questions are likely to appear on the test. Aggressive test taking, then, begins with an effort to gather information about the sample of questions the instructor will use to judge your total knowledge.

TESTS AS MEASURING DEVICES

A second issue about tests is how well a test measures what has been sampled. In other words, are the questions on a test a good measure of what you know? A good test is difficult to construct. For example, to measure what you know, a test should be carefully constructed to cover a broad range of ability. By including both difficult and easy questions, the instructor has a better opportunity to make an accurate statement about your knowledge and ability, which could range from very poor to very good. If a test contained only difficult questions that could be answered only by exceptional students, then the test would give no indication of what good, average, or poor students know. Likewise, very easy tests give you little opportunity to distinguish yourself as being an exceptional student.

As with the sampling problem, we know that all teachers are not equally able to construct tests that measure a broad range of knowledge. The aggressive test taker should recognize that tests vary in how accurately knowledge is measured. All tests should be viewed as imperfect measuring devices. In addition to the problem of test difficulty, such other characteristics as questions with many meanings, poor directions, and time constraints contribute to inaccurate measurement. Later, we will explain how aggressive test takers who understand these problems can actually take advantage of test imperfections to demonstrate what they know.

TEACHERS' MOTIVES FOR GIVING TESTS

Another important factor you should understand is that, although teachers clearly test to see what you know, they vary in their motives for giving tests. Although all teachers want to find out what you know, there are at least two strategies that may be used to measure your knowledge. One is to see what you have learned, and the other is to see what you have not learned. There are important differences between these two approaches.

A teacher who wants to find out what you have learned will ask relatively straightforward questions directly related to the main purposes of the course. This teacher wants to probe your knowledge about some clearly stated course purposes or objectives. The teacher is not interested in separating the best student from the less able. Determining how you are progressing toward course objectives is the teacher's concern. Most teachers who give tests to find out what you have learned will not "grade on the curve" or adjust grades.

Teachers who want to determine what you have not learned will ask at least some relatively difficult questions (some of these will be referred to as "picky" questions), a few of which may not seem related to major course purposes. The teachers who are interested in selecting the "best" students often curve grades. That is, the students with the highest scores will get high grades regardless of their actual score. Some teachers will attempt to measure both what you have learned and what you have not learned by asking a broad range of questions, but adjusting scores either up or down to determine grades. The way you study and take tests should depend on which motive your instructor has for giving tests.[1]

DEMONSTRATING WHAT YOU KNOW

From the perspective of a student then, what is it you want to do when you take a test? Clearly, you want to demonstrate what you know. Frequently, students who get the best grades do not know more than the others, they just use better the knowledge they have. Several important features of tests may make it more or less difficult to demonstrate your knowledge. We will briefly describe these in order to stress the need to become an aggressive test taker and to use appropriate test-taking strategies.

---

[1]Test grades frequently reflect more than your answers to questions on the test. Class participation, seat location, promptness, even dress have all been shown to affect test grades. You may think that only your answer should determine test grades, but professors, being human, are consciously or unconsciously affected by their own images of the good student. Suggestions for enhancing your image are presented throughout the book, particularly in Chapter 7.

First, psychologists and educational researchers have devoted years to the study of testing and test construction. This research has produced much information that teachers may use to prepare tests to measure student learning. Tests written using this knowledge are generally fair and reliable; this means the test is a good way to measure what students know. If your teacher is aware of this research information and uses it wisely, you can be pretty sure that you are getting a good test.[2]

Tests created by teachers who are unaware of the information on how to construct good tests will sometimes contain questions that are misleading or appear to be unrelated to the content of the course. These poor questions make it very difficult for students to demonstrate what they know. However, if your professor writes the questions, he or she also decides which answers are correct. Thus, as an aggressive test taker, you can deal with misleading questions by discussing them with the instructor during the test or after.

Another problem is that tests are often not scored or corrected in a uniform manner. This is particularly true for essay tests, but also true for so-called objective tests, such as multiple-choice tests. It is often possible to improve test grades by explaining the reason for your answer or by pointing out the possibility of having misunderstood the question. Again, we will give some suggestions in the subsequent chapters on ways to improve tests scores.

Our purpose in describing these principles on test taking is to help you understand that a test may or may not accurately measure what you know. Tests are made up by human beings and as a result may contain some flaws. If you understand these problems and know how to work around them, then you have a much better chance of getting a better grade. Every type of test has certain unique characteristics; if you understand these characteristics, then you can use the actions we will suggest to improve your test scores.

In the following chapters, we describe test characteristics and strategies for the most commonly used kinds of tests. This information will help you understand the purposes of each test and the test-taking strategies for each. By reviewing the test-taking strategies before taking a test, you will combine your knowledge *and* effective test-taking skills to get the best score you can on every test. This will make you an aggressive test taker.

In addition to chapters on taking tests, we have included some principles for studying or preparing for tests. These are principles that we believe apply to every test. Consider how you can use these principles as you study. To assist you in making these action principles a regular part of your test taking, we have included some action practice activities at the end of each chapter.

---

[2]The following are several sources that summarize accepted test construction techniques in a readable format: G. Sax, *Principles of Educational and Psychological Measurement and Evaluation* (Belmont, Cal.: Wadsworth Publishing Co., 1980); C. M. Lindvall, *Measuring Pupil Achievement and Aptitudes* (New York: Harcourt, Brace & World, 1967); N. E. Gronlund, *Measurement and Evaluation of Teaching*, 3d ed. (New York: Macmillan, 1976); T. D. TenBrink, *Evaluation: A Practical Guide for Teachers* (New York: McGraw-Hill, 1974).

Being an aggressive and effective test taker requires some effort. However, usually no additional time is required when compared to your regular study habits. If anything, you may find that less time is needed for study when the suggestions in this book are followed.

We have also included some ways you can present yourself as a serious and dedicated student to your teachers. Of course, you must want to learn and to try to learn. However, if your teacher does not perceive you as a serious student, your intent to be serious may not yield the benefits of high test scores. Again, practice these principles and use them. It is not a matter of making a greater effort as much as making your efforts count.

Most importantly, remember that you are making yourself into an aggressive test taker. Believe in yourself and your ability to demonstrate what you know. All of us have a lot of knowledge; yet, most of us do not use this knowledge wisely when we take tests. Confidence in your ability to do well on tests comes from recognizing what you know and knowing how to use your knowledge to your best advantage. The principles included in the rest of this book will help you gain the confidence that you can use your knowledge to get better test scores.

USING THIS BOOK

Each chapter in this book follows the same pattern. An introduction describes what the chapter covers; specific action principles are presented; the chapter is summarized or reviewed; and some practice exercises are given. We have used this method of organization because (1) material written in this way is usually easier to learn and remember, and (2) each chapter may be used separately. You may review the material in any chapter by reading only the introduction and summary. If you need more information, you can easily find it by referring directly to the principles included in the Table of Contents. So, you may use this book to refresh your memory as well as to learn.

We have included examples from many different subjects to illustrate the action principles described. It is impossible to include an example from every subject; most examples are from introductory courses in science, English, and history. These are the courses almost all students must take when they begin college. Use the examples in this book to help you find other examples from your own tests. We suggest that you actually look at some tests you have been given to see how you can apply the action principles. Applying these principles is very important for learning, remembering, and using the principles to get good grades.

Finally, at the end of each chapter are some action practice exercises. These should help you to check how well you have mastered the principles in the chapter. But you need to do more than only these practice exercises. You need to think about taking tests and create examples of how you can use these

8

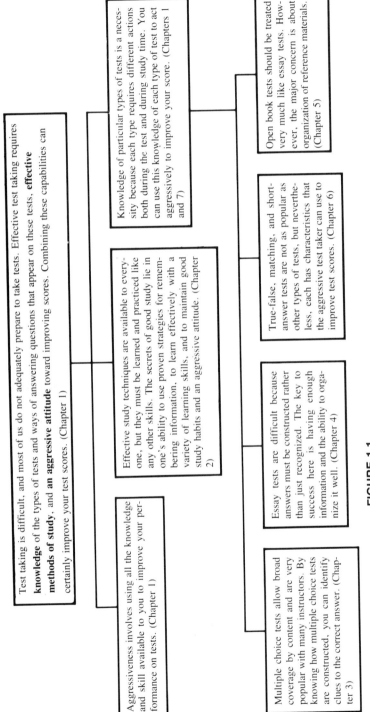

Test taking is difficult, and most of us do not adequately prepare to take tests. Effective test taking requires **knowledge** of the types of tests and ways of answering questions that appear on these tests, **effective methods of study**, and **an aggressive attitude** toward improving scores. Combining these capabilities can certainly improve your test scores. (Chapter 1)

Aggressiveness involves using all the knowledge and skill available to you to improve your performance on tests. (Chapter 1)

Effective study techniques are available to everyone, but they must be learned and practiced like any other skills. The secrets of good study lie in one's ability to use proven strategies for remembering information, to learn effectively with a variety of learning skills, and to maintain good study habits and an aggressive attitude. (Chapter 2)

Knowledge of particular types of tests is a necessity because each type requires different actions both during the test and during study time. You can use this knowledge of each type of test to act aggressively to improve your score. (Chapters 1 and 7)

Multiple choice tests allow broad coverage by content and are very popular with many instructors. By knowing how multiple choice tests are constructed, you can identify clues to the correct answer. (Chapter 3)

Essay tests are difficult because answers must be constructed rather than just recognized. The key to success here is having enough information and the ability to organize it well. (Chapter 4)

True-false, matching, and short-answer tests are not as popular as other types of tests, but nevertheless, each has characteristics that the aggressive test taker can use to improve test scores. (Chapter 6)

Open book tests should be treated very much like essay tests. However, the major concern is about organization of reference materials. (Chapter 5)

FIGURE 1.1
A Summary of How to Be a Successful Test Taker

ideas. You need to actively and aggressively use these ideas when you take tests. These principles must be practiced to improve your test scores. The practice exercises will help you practice, but you must use the principles with your own tests, past and future, to make yourself an aggressive test taker.

A summary of the information on how to be a successful test taker presented in this book is given in Figure1.1. If you read over this summary and see how this information fits together, it will help you learn the principles.

Action Practice

Here are some practice questions to review chapter 1.

Short Answer

1. Aggressive test takers attack tests with confidence by taking two kinds of action.

   a.

   b.

2. What does it mean to say tests *sample* your knowledge?

3. What are two motives teachers have for giving tests?
   a.

b.

4. What is your main goal as a student when you take a test?

5. How can you become an aggressive test taker?

True-False

_____ 1. Taking tests is so simple that we do not need to learn *how* to take tests.

_____ 2. Good test grades are a matter of luck.

_____ 3. You can improve your ability to get good test grades by using action principles.

_____ 4. A good test score depends only on how much you know.

_____ 5. It is éasy for teachers to make up good tests.

_____ 6. Tests are always good measuring devices.

_____ 7. Some tests will *not* be good measures of your knowledge.

_____ 8. You should prepare for a test by predicting what will appear on a test.

Answers

Short Answer

1. Preparing for tests
   Learning how to take tests

2. The questions on a test will cover only a portion of your knowledge. From this sample, the teacher will infer how much you have learned.

If you can predict the sample your teacher will test, you can improve your ability to get good test scores.

3. To see what students know
   To see what students do not know

4. To demonstrate what you know

5. Becoming an aggressive test taker requires an understanding of the reasons teachers give tests, the characteristics of tests, and learning how to be a skilled test taker. Developing test-taking skills includes knowing why teachers choose different types of tests, how to prepare for tests, and principles for effectively taking tests. This knowledge and these principles make it possible to attack tests aggressively and to maximize test scores by using knowledge well.

True-False

1. F
2. F
3. T
4. F
5. F
6. F
7. T
8. T

Preparing for Tests

Most of your studying will be for tests. Yet many students do not study specifically for the test they will be given. Instead, they study by reading textbooks and reviewing class notes in a general way, often trying to remember everything they read. Many students also use the same study methods for every test and every subject. Clearly, it is important to study before taking a test if you want to do well. But just spending time with your books and notes will not always result in high test grades. Successful students focus their study and use special study skills to get good grades. In this chapter, we will show you how to focus your study so that you will learn more of the information you study and increase your ability to do well on tests.

Specifically, we will present study principles to help you focus your study efforts as you read textbooks and class notes. We will also describe how you can improve your memory so you can remember what you have studied. Finally, we will tell you how successful students prepare themselves for tests so they do not get nervous or upset about having to take tests.

LEARNING ABOUT TESTS

Principle 2.1: Get information about the test.

The first step in successfully studying for a test is to learn as much as you can about the test you will take. This will allow you to focus your study on important issues and use your study time wisely. In each of the following chapters, we will urge you to find out what information a test will cover, what kinds of questions will be asked, and the sources (books, notes, etc.) the questions will cover. This information will make it possible for you to study for the test you will be given.

When you know you will have a test, you should ask the following questions:

- When will the test be given?
- What type of questions will be asked?
- What content or information will be on the test?
- What sources (textbook, outside readings, class) will test questions cover?
- What do I need to know to do well on the test?

You should be able to answer all of these questions specifically. For example, you should know the exact date of the test and the time. Content should be described in specific terms, such as "Digestion in simpler animals, digestion in man, and digestion in plants," rather than just "digestion." You also want to know if the test will include essay questions, multiple-choice questions, or other types of questions. Identify the exact pages, chapters, and days of class to be included on the test. It is much easier to study a section of a book than the whole book.

Finally, find out what you must know in the books or your notes to do well on the test. It is impossible to remember everything you study, even when only a small amount of material is included. If you can focus your study efforts on limited material, you will be able to learn better than if you have to cover a lot of material. You can find out what you must know by asking your teacher, paying attention to what is emphasized in class, and using review or study questions in your textbook. Again, you want to be specific, so ask questions like: "Will we have to know the digestion process?" "Will we have to know experiments done on digestion?" and so forth. Find out specific topics and issues in the chapters and class notes to focus your study.

STUDY SKILLS

Once you have found out the basic information about a test, you are ready to begin your study. Most good students are successful because they know how to study well. Studying is something you must do for yourself; it is a self-directed activity. You must aggressively take charge of your study, directing and controlling your use of study skills so that you will learn more and get good test scores. In this section, we will show you how to direct your study.

Characteristics of Effective Study

Let us begin by looking at five important characteristics of effective, aggressive students.

Active involvement. The first thing noticeable about good students is that they are *actively involved* in their study. They read actively, listen actively, concentrate, and pay attention. For many of us, it is difficult to understand how to maintain this active involvement. It is so easy to let our thoughts wander, rather than to pay attention. There are two parts to active study: believing that your study will help you do well on a test and recognizing that you can understand what you read.

Effective study, which is directed toward specific learning goals and follows a study plan, results in better learning and may take less time than your previous method. As you plan and direct your study, consider three types of activities: activities that prepare you to study, study activities, and activities that follow study. These study activities will help you become an *active* learner.

Recognizing that you can understand the material. Many of us get discouraged when we fail to understand something we are studying. Most of the time we *can* understand if we *change* our study activity. For example, many students highlight or underline as they read. This is their main study activity. When this does not work to improve understanding, they are lost. Frequently, these students will try to improve their understanding by underlining more and more of what they read. Usually this will not help at all. These students need to use a *different* study activity to improve their understanding. Do not be fooled into thinking you cannot understand some material because it is difficult or because you did not understand it the first time you tried. Recognizing that you do not understand usually means you need to use a stronger study activity. We describe many of these study activities in the following sections. If one study activity does not work, you can try others. But be assured that you can understand if you use these study activities.

Relating the material. Another thing good students do is relate what they are studying to what they already know. You know how much easier it is to study for a test in a subject you know well. One reason it is easier to learn new information in such a situation is that you already know a lot about what you are studying. It is much easier to expand knowledge than to learn new subjects. When studying, successful students look for ways that new knowledge can be related to what they already know, thereby making studying much easier. The study activities we describe will include several principles to help you relate what you study to what you already know.

Interest. Lack of interest in the material studied is probably the main cause of poor test grades. Low interest makes active attention difficult and makes expanding what is already known impossible. Lack of interest is also the main reason students stop studying before they understand the material. Good students develop and maintain their interest. And they have interest in all the courses they take, not just the ones they naturally like. There are several ways to develop interest in a subject. For example, getting good grades, relating course information to career goals, and developing positive attitudes about school and study are all ways you can develop interest and positive attitudes about study. These and some other activities to develop interest will be described.

Self-testing. A final, significant characteristic of effective students is that they often *test themselves* on what they are studying. They do this by asking themselves questions, asking questions in class, asking questions of other students, making up possible test questions, and using review and study questions in textbooks. Good students are rarely content with only reading or reviewing material to prepare for a test. Instead, they frequently test themselves, looking for what they understand and noting what they fail to understand. We will also describe how to test your own knowledge and understanding.

Preparation Study Skills

The following study activities will help you increase what you learn from your study. All of these skills are usually used by successful students as they study.

Principle 2.2: Set study goals.

Study goals are developed to help focus your study. These goals may come from several sources, but *you* must decide what *your* goals are. These goals should describe what you must learn to be successful on a test.

How should you develop goals? One way is to use questions in your textbook, study guide, or old tests from the class. Another way to choose goals is to use course or class objectives. A third way is to use major points stressed in class. You should always write down your study goals so you can check yourself to see that you have met them. Your goals should be very specific. "I'm going to learn this chapter" is *not* a good goal. "I will learn the answers to the first ten study questions at the end of the chapter" *is* a good goal. "I will learn the meaning of the following terms . . ." *is* a good goal. "I will understand psychology" is *not* a good goal; it is too broad and not specific. "I will understand the theory of B. F. Skinner" is a better goal. And, "I will understand reinforcement, punishment, and schedules" *is* a good goal because it is specific.

Goals should cover three kinds of learning: facts, comparisons, and relationships. Later, we will describe these types of learning. For now, we want you to recognize that when you set goals for your study you must include goals to guide your study in learning everything that is important for a test.

Good goals let you focus your study on the specific information you need to know to do well on a test. Focused study usually results in good test scores. Setting study goals is the first step in focusing your study, increasing your interest, and testing yourself.

Principle 2.3: Survey first.

All effective study is preceded by what is called a survey. Surveying means looking over the material before you study. You want to get an idea of what you will study before you actually study. Surveying allows you to judge how much of the information you already know and how much time you will need to study. You can also judge your level of interest. You can survey information in at least three ways:

Look at headings. Look at text headings and subheadings, titles, graphs, pictures, and highlighted words. Look for familiar and unfamiliar terms and how difficult the material looks. With unfamiliar material, you may want to turn headings and subheadings into questions. For example, the subheading "Standard Deviation" could be made into the questions "What is a standard deviation?" "Why is it standard?" "What kinds of deviation are not standard?" "How is a standard deviation computed?" and "What are the uses of standard deviations?"

Look at summary sections and questions. Most textbooks contain summaries at the beginning and the end of each chapter. Also, major sections of a chapter will usually have brief summaries. The first and last lines of each paragraph often are summaries of the material in the paragraph. Reading over these summary sections can provide you with more detailed information about the material in the chapter. As you read these summaries, look for information you recognize, and ask questions that you think you must answer to understand the material. Relate what you read to what you already know by asking yourself questions like: "How does this information relate to the information in the previous section or chapter?" "Can I think of anything in my daily life similar to this material?" "How will knowing this information help me meet my career goals?" "What is there in this chapter that relates to a special interest of mine?"

Read larger portions of the text. You may read a whole paragraph, for example, or a whole section. Reading larger sections can provide you with more information about what you will study. As with the other two survey techniques, relate the material to your own knowledge by asking questions. See how much you already know and how you can relate the material to your interests.

Principle 2.4: Prepare study questions.

A good way to focus your study is to have questions you must answer to understand the material. These questions should be about the material you read and may come from several places.

Make up questions. As you survey, you can make up questions about things you don't understand. Write these questions on a study sheet; later, as you read, you can write down the answer. Write questions that cover facts, relationships, and comparisons.

Predict test questions. Possible test questions are an excellent guide to focus study. Use old tests by reading over the questions and predicting answers. Then, as you read, look for answers to the questions. Pay particular attention to questions requiring more than a factual answer.

Use listed objectives and study questions. Many textbooks include a list of objectives or purposes at the beginning of a chapter. You may change these into questions or use them as they appear in the book. Your goal when you study is to meet these objectives. Many teachers will begin a lecture with objectives; use these to help you listen to the lecture just as you use written objectives to help you read. A second source of questions is study questions, review questions, or practice exercises found in textbooks. Students who answer these questions get higher grades than students who do not. Many textbooks also have study guides that include questions in addition to other study aids.

Whether you get questions from only one or all three sources, or from some other source (e.g., a fellow student) you should write down the answer to these questions. Students who write down an answer, or at a minimum, say the answer to a fellow student or the teacher, get higher test grades.

Principle 2.5: Plan your study time.

Learning can sometimes appear to be a monumental task. As with any management activity, managing your study time and activities requires planning. This planning can make studying and learning appear much more realistic for you. We suggest you plan your study time in three ways:

Plan how much material to cover. Consider many factors in this decision, such as how long before the test, how much other work must be done, how difficult is the material, how difficult will the test be, how much do you already know, and any other important matter. For example, if you have ten days to study 200 pages, simply studying 20 pages a day may not be sufficient. You must plan for review time and such study activities as surveying and questioning.

Plan how much time you will spend. Time can be divided many ways. How you schedule your time can have a big impact on test grades. Doing all your studying right before a test ("cramming") is *not* a good idea. However, a concentrated *review* session right before a test *is* a good idea. Studying for short periods, ten to twenty minutes, is *not* a good idea. Studying for long sessions, sixty to ninety minutes, *is* a good idea. Spacing your study sessions *is* a good idea; study for an hour or two each day rather than four or five hours every two or three days. The best study schedule includes regular study (daily) for an hour or two for many days, ending with a concentrated review session just before a test.

Plan how the time will be used. You must manage many study activities; so it is important to schedule the use of these activities. Large portions of early study time may be devoted to survey activities, planning, and questioning. Later study periods may be devoted to reading or review activities. You must decide how to use your study time; make a schedule of activities and stick to it. Learning does not just happen, you must plan to make learning happen.

We suggest you establish a routine of activities that you always use. One example of a good routine follows:

- Briefly review previously studied material (survey notes or texts and study questions).
- Survey new material to be studied.
- Make up or review study questions.
- Study material.
- Review material studied.

A routine such as this will allow you to concentrate and focus your study regularly. With practice, you can use this routine easily and effectively in the same way you learned to drive a car or any other regular activity.

These four study activities, setting goals, surveying, questioning, and planning, are essential study skills. Aggressive use and management of these skills by you will increase the amount you learn from your study time. The next section describes how you can use these study activities to read and study notes for tests.

STUDY SKILLS FOR LEARNING WITH CONFIDENCE

The majority of the information you will study for tests comes from two places—books and class notes. As you study books and notes, it is important that you know you are learning the ideas and information you will need for your test. This is learning with confidence. You can become confident by controlling and using specific study skills as you study for your test.

Principle 2.6: Read for main ideas.

The first goal in reading books and notes is to find the main ideas. As you read, frequently ask yourself questions about what you read. These may be questions from your preparation study skills, or they may be questions that occur to you while you read. As you read, stop occasionally to ask yourself these questions:

1. Does this information answer any questions that I have already asked or that appear on sample tests, study guides, or class notes?
2. What is the author's main point? Can I restate it in a sentence or two?
3. Do I understand what the author is saying?
4. Can I restate what the author is saying in my own words?

Answer these questions to yourself in detail. Do not just think ''Yes, I can'' and read on. Actually try to restate what the author has written, as well as your teacher's ideas found in your notes.

This procedure is sometimes called active reading. An active reader stops reading the words and thinks about what has been read after every two or three paragraphs. Think of what you know about, what you read, and how the new information adds to what you already know. You may find that you do not know how the information relates to what you already know, or that you cannot restate what you have read in your own words. This discovery is not necessarily bad; it means you need to develop some new questions that can be answered by rereading the material.

You should never read for long periods of time without understanding.

Understanding is something that will not come automatically just because you have read every word on every page. You must make the information have meaning by searching through it for the main ideas. The best way to do this is to use your study questions and restate the author's ideas in your own words. Everyone, even very exceptional students, has to reread from time to time.

Principle 2.7: Regularly test your confidence.

As you study, regularly check to see how well you know what you are studying. There are six techniques for doing this:

See how you "feel" about the material. Most students can fairly accurately judge if they know what they are studying. They "feel" good about what they have learned because they can answer study questions and accurately restate what they have read. Test your own feelings often. If you feel good, read on; if not, review the material.

Write out a summary of what you have studied. Writing is important, since this allows you to reread what you have written. If you only think about it, you cannot check what you think. Include the main ideas and some details of what you read in these summaries.

Discuss the material with other students. Ask other students what they thought the main points were, and describe what you think they are. If you find that others have different ideas, write these down and reread to check your ideas.

Reread the material for any problems you have in understanding. If you can't answer some questions or have trouble restating, look for new ideas that will help you understand these problems as you reread.

Read additional material. If you don't understand some material, read other sections in the book or notes that cover the same topic. Look in the index to find these sections; read them actively to answer your problems. Do not worry if the sections occur before or after the specific section you are reading.

Make a list of items, issues, or ideas you do not understand. Use this list as a study guide. Ask these questions in class, ask your professor privately, or ask other students.

MAKING LEARNING STICK

Good students do not just stop studying. Instead, they reflect and act upon the material just read. Thinking over what you have read immediately after reading is one of the best ways to make sure you will recall at test time. The following principles include activities that will help you improve your understanding and ability to remember.

Principle 2.8: Solidify learning by summarizing.

One of the most important things you can do to help you on a test is to actively summarize what you have studied. These summaries should be relatively short, but should cover all the material you have studied. Here are two activities to help you make your learning stick:

Write a general summary. Think of yourself as having to write a summary paragraph of the text material or your teacher's lecture. You must write this on paper and review it after it is written. You can compare your summary with the author's. Another way to do this is to think of having to teach the class yourself. What would you tell the class was the main purpose of the class? What would you teach them?

Develop a study and review guide. This should include all the important ideas, dates, places, and so on, and page numbers where they can be found. Each of these should be related to the main ideas included in the section studied.

Using good study skills does not usually require more study time. It does require using your time in different ways. You should always use a variety of study skills. You will learn more if you do. When you don't understand, you must switch to a different activity that will help you understand. Difficult material will require more time than easy material. But you can learn the material if you manage and control how you study by selecting the best study skill for the material that will be on a test. You have a variety of skills to choose from; if one doesn't work, try another.

MEMORY: IMPROVING YOUR ABILITY TO REMEMBER

If you study effectively, you remember what you have learned for a test. However, even with the most effective study, test scores can be improved by improving your ability to remember what you study. Your memory can be increased if you actively and aggressively manage memory skills. Before we present these skills, we will take a moment to help you understand how your memory works and how you can help yourself remember more of what you study.

We have stressed the need to manage your learning. You can also manage your memory. Our memories are like filing systems—if information is filed by alphabetical order or by categories, the information will be found more easily.

You can think about your own memory as a file cabinet. If you are careless about how you put information in, you will have trouble getting it out. For example, you may have taken a test sometime in which you felt sure that you had the answer to a question, but could not recall it. If you are careful about how you put information into your memory, you will be amazed at how easily you can remember a large amount of detail. *Organization* is the key to remembering.

Principle 2.9: Organize the information you must remember.

Organizing what you want to remember requires active management on your part. There are many ways to organize files in your memory. The following examples are but a few of these. Most people use one or two different ways to organize information.

Textbook topics. Every textbook is organized by topics. These topics are usually printed in type that is different from the regular type. These topics can be thought of as file folders in your memory that hold information. You can remember the information by first thinking of the topic and then "looking" in the file for more specific information.

Hierarchical schemes. In political science, for example, descriptions of small elements of government are organized under larger elements, which are themselves organized under yet larger units until, finally, at the very top of the structure, a single statement is found that states what government is.

Thematic schemes. Knowledge in literature and in history, to name but two disciplines, often follows a thematic organization. In history, for example, the early development of this country can be traced through the themes of bold exploration, political ambition, religious upheaval, or economic rivalry among major European powers. Each theme might give a somewhat different picture, but, with a theme, a consistent view of colonial development can be constructed.

Organization by function. When studying dynamic organizations and structures, information may be organized by the function characteristic of the different elements. In government, for example, function may be used to organize because the meaning of such subunits as judicial and legislative bodies lies in the functions they perform. An additional example is biology, in which many life systems (e.g., the circulatory system) are organized around functions, such as supply, cooling, and healing.

Organization by structure. Sometimes content is best understood in terms of its structure as in

> Structure of chemical bonds
> Structure of government organizations
> Structure of social systems in animals and humans
> Structure of cells in biology
> Structure of political systems
> Structure of crystals in geology

Organization by theory. Perhaps one of the more complex and abstract ways to organize is by theory. All subjects have theories that are attempts to describe and explain the subject. Examine some of your textbooks dealing with the basic underlying thought of what you are studying to see how many times theory is used to organize discussion about the subject.

Principle 2.10: Use memory techniques or tricks.

In addition to careful organization, there are some techniques memory experts use to help them remember. Some of the techniques are good for remembering only limited amounts of information, such as names and dates. Other techniques are more useful for recalling main ideas. Many memory experts use more than one technique.

Overlearning. Regardless of how much we study, we will forget some of what we learn. As a general rule, however, the more we study a single topic, the less of it we will forget. Once you feel you know what you are studying, you can "overlearn" by continuing to study. The more you study after you have mastered the material, the more you will remember. This technique is good for improving your ability to remember anything.

Analogies. An analogy is comparing one thing to another. We have used several analogies to help you understand and remember in this book (e.g., an aggressive test taker is like an aggressive driver, and the memory is like a file cabinet). These analogies assist us in remembering important ideas about test taking. Another analogy students sometimes use is to think of the relationship between colonial America and England as a parent-child relationship. To create an analogy, you want to compare what you want to remember to something you already know.

Images. One of the most powerful memory techniques is to create a mental picture of what you want to remember. To be most effective, you should try to "see" the picture in your mind. These mental pictures do not have to be realistic and may be quite unusual. Apparently, just trying to create a picture will help remember the content of the picture.

Loci method. *Loci* means place. To use this method, memorize a series of locations, such as the rooms in your house. Then, mentally place the information to be remembered in various rooms. For example, if you are remembering the peoples of Eastern Europe in the early 20th century, you could mentally place each group in a different room. The Slavs could be placed in the bathroom with the salve; the Croats in the closet with the coats; the Bulgars in the garage with the Buick, and so forth. To recall these peoples for a test, you can mentally walk through your house.

Rhymes. Such rhymes as "thirty days has September, April, June, and November . . ." can remind you of factual information. Creating rhymes like this can assist you in remembering facts. Here is a rhyme to help you remember the seven principles on study skills:

Goals, Survey, Quest,
Plan, Ideas, Test
and Summarize

If you can make up rhymes, they will help you remember details and main facts.

Acronyms. An acronym is formed by using the first letter or two of words in a longer statement. We use an acronym later in this book to help you remember how to take essay tests. Acronyms can be real or made-up words. A famous acronym used to help remember trigonometry information is SOH CAH TOA (Sine = Opposite/Hypotenuse; Cosine = Adjacent/Hypotenuse; Tangent = Opposite/Adjacent). You can make up acronyms to help you remember any information.

Recitation/rehearsal. If you repeat, aloud, many times, the information you wish to remember, you will improve your ability to remember. The information you rehearse should be short and concise; if it also rhymes and is connected to a mental picture, it will be even easier to remember.

Restating. We have mentioned restating before as a study skill, but it is also a way to improve your memory. On several occasions, restate in writing the information you wish to remember. Restating can help you remember anything, but particularly should be helpful in recalling main ideas.

Intend to remember. Psychologists have found that intending or wanting to remember is important. If you study with the intention to recall, your intention must be *active*, rather than a passive wish. Wishing takes no action or work; intending requires activity. You can actively intend to remember by using the techniques described above and the study skills described in the previous section.

Most of these memory techniques do not require much time or effort. Best of all, they give you actions you can take to improve your memory. When using these techniques, remember that no facts or information should be studied in isolation. These techniques can help you remember information in the files of your memory. Because the memory depends on organization, your first task to improve memory is to organize the information you will need for a test.

Here is one final hint on remembering. Frequently, we will think we know something, but will be unable to recall it. Sometimes we say, "I've got it on the tip of my tongue." This information can usually be remembered if we try to reconstruct or rebuild our memory. Reconstruction is done by recalling information about what we want to remember. For example, you are trying to remember the details of a story. Instead of thinking only about the story, try to remember *where* you read the story, what you were *wearing*, what you did *before* you read and *after*. Did anything you read make you think of *something else* you were doing? Usually, thinking like this will help you recall a few details, and thinking about those details will help you recall more details. Finally, you reconstruct the whole story.

PREPARING FOR DIFFERENT TEST EXPECTATIONS

We all know tests can be quite different. They may require repeating many facts, comparing events or ideas, or solving a problem. Test expectations are different because not all teachers expect students to learn the same things. Because teachers' expectations vary, we stated in Principle 2.1, Get Some Information About the Test. In this section, we want to help you understand the types of learning teachers will expect in order to focus your study on the type of learning *your* professor will expect.

Each type of learning requires different study skills and preparation. In the following chapters, we will point out how different forms of tests (multiple choice, essay, etc.) usually measure different types of learning. For now, we want you to see what these different types of learning are.

Look at Table 2.1; it contains five columns. The first column lists three different types of learning: information, manipulating information, and problem solving. In the second column are general requirements that correspond to the types of learning. To further assist you in organizing different expectations for tests, the third column lists some verbs that are usually used by teachers to indicate their expectations. The next column presents some examples of questions for each type of learning. Column five includes some study activities you may use to help you prepare for each type of learning.

You may use this table to help you prepare for tests by locating the type of learning you will have to demonstrate on a test. If you have some sample questions, look in column four for questions similar to the sample questions. You can then locate general requirements and study activities most appropriate for that test. However, remember that you should never study only by trying to memorize. Even though some types of learning require remembering facts, you must organize your facts into your memory to remember them for a test. The following paragraphs describe these types of learning in more detail.

Probably, most test questions will come from Type I, which involves obtaining and remembering information. For both requirements under Type I, you have to recognize and/or repeat facts, concepts, or generalizations you have learned exactly as you learned them. There is, however, a big difference between verbatim recall (IA) and comprehension (IB). Verbatim recall is mostly rote learning or memorization. This is not especially difficult, but is hard to remember for a long time unless these facts are related to something you know well.

Comprehending information, however, is a different matter. As noted in Table 2.1, comprehension requires information be put into your own words. You must be able to recognize or produce the details in a different way than how you studied. If we wanted to test your comprehension, we would ask questions like "Can you tell me in your own words?" "What does _____ mean?" "How is _____ like _____?" and so forth. Usually, if you can repeat something accurately in your own words, you have comprehended it.

The second general type of learning, manipulating information, requires that a larger body of information be manipulated. In the first case (IIA), you must demonstrate a skill called analysis—breaking a body of information into its parts. Generally, you will see questions like "Let's take this thing apart and see how it works." As shown in Table 2.1, analysis is often called for when you are asked to compare and contrast, discriminate between, identify the elements of, or answer such questions as "What went wrong here?" Exactly the opposite activity is required in the second (IIB). Here you must produce something using the material you studied. It should be easy to see from the

TABLE 2.1
Types of Learning Frequently Found in Tests

Types of Learning	General Requirement	Verbs Describing Specific Actions	Example of Questions	Preparation
I. Information A.	Verbatim recall of information, remembering word for word	Describe, list, name	"Who wrote . . ." "List the five parts of . . ." "Name the person who . . ."	Memory for facts and detail
B.	Comprehension of information requires ability to understand and produce information in own words.	Explain, paraphrase, estimate, convert, summarize	"Describe how to . . ." "Summarize briefly the meaning of . . ." "Explain how . . ."	Restating accurately
II. Manipulating Information A.	Ability to take some body of information such as a story, a procedure, or a plan and identify the individual elements and/or the relationships among the elements. This kind of learning is often called analysis.	Identify, point out, separate, subdivide, discriminate, differentiate, compare	"Point out the differences between democracy and communism." "Identify the essential elements of the plan." "Differentiate between process A and process B."	Restating, memory of detail, major emphasis on main ideas, organization
B.	Ability to form new products from individual parts, such as in designing a building, writing a story, preparing a lesson, or generating an accounting system. This kind of learning is often called synthesis.	Compose, construct, plan, organize, design, rewrite, describe	"Construct a plan to . . ." "Organize a theme around the idea of . . ." "Construct an argument that we can present at the next meeting."	Restating, organization, detail, analogies, images, extensive thinking about ideas
III. Solving Problems A.	Involves routine application of information (e.g., substituting numbers from a math problem into a formula).	Solve, compute, demonstrate, show, use, predict	"Given this list, what is the average score?" "Use these data to predict next month's rainfall." "What is the legal solution here?"	Memory of formulas, procedures, detail
B.	Involves the ability to combine previously learned concepts and rules to solve a new or novel problem.	generate, find out, devise, invent, come up with, explain	"Devise a way to . . ." "How do you explain the unusual situation that arose when . . ." "Here is a situation, how . . ."	Restating, organization, analogies, images

examples in Table 2.1 that there are several different activities you could be asked to perform on a test. Your ability to do well on a test will depend on how well you studied and prepared for this kind of question.

Finally, problem solving is the kind of activity the most of your professors would like to teach you. We have listed two types of problem solving behaviors. The first (IIIA) is a practical application activity. Here, you are typically asked to solve problems similar to ones you have seen before. For example, in a mathematics course, you may be asked to use a particular theorem to solve a problem that is like others you have seen. On the other hand, if the problem requires a new and unusual use of the theorem, then this constitutes a much more difficult problem and thus fits the type IIIB category.

Some expectations are clearly more difficult than others. What we would like to see you do is to discover just what your instructor has in mind. If requirements are not given in the form of objectives, then make it your business to ask. You can study much more effectively and efficiently if you know what to expect.

How should you study for each type of learning? To help you tailor your study, we have included a list of general study questions for each type of requirement. Use these questions with the other study skills to focus your study better.

I. Information

Have I taken all possible steps to organize individual facts into a summary?

Can I relate this information to something I already know?

Is it possible to develop a memory technique for this information?

II. Manipulating Information

Do I really know how this procedure (story, plan, design, etc.) works? Let's see if I can take it apart and examine the parts. How do the individual elements compare to other organizations that are familiar?

Can I create a new way of doing this? Can I think of new applications? Could I create something like that myself?

III. Problem Solving

Do I understand how this information (formula, etc.) was used in class?

Have I practiced using this material instead of just repeating it over and over?

Can I solve practice problems?

How many ways can I think of to use this information?

Have I practiced solving unusual problems?

DEVELOPING THE BEST ATTITUDE TO TAKE A TEST

A positive attitude is important for getting good test grades. You must believe in yourself and your ability to do well on a test. Do not think of a test as something to show, or to trick you into showing, ignorance. Think of a test as an *opportunity* to demonstrate what you have learned through your hard work. One thing that can get in the way of believing in yourself is worry. In this section, we will describe how you can control anxiety about tests.

The first step in controlling anxiety is recognizing that worrying about tests is normal. All good students are concerned about tests; this anxiety motivates study. Psychologists who have studied anxiety have concluded that some anxiety is good. In fact, students with some anxiety usually get higher test grades than students with no anxiety. However, too much anxiety usually means poor test scores.

If you believe you have too much anxiety, you can take action to reduce your anxiety. The following are indicators of too much anxiety:

1. You study using the suggestions and principles included in this book and still get low test scores.
2. You feel sick, dizzy, nervous, and/or afraid before taking a test.
3. You do well on all homework assignments, but never do well on tests.
4. You "feel" you know the material and can discuss the test topics with other students but "freeze up" or your "mind goes blank" when you have a test.

Test anxiety is quite common in students and is relatively easily controlled. We will give you some suggestions on how to mentally develop a good, positive attitude for test taking. However, if you think you have test anxiety, contact your school's counselor for more help in overcoming the problem. If you are unsure of what to say to the counselor, take this book with you to help explain your feelings about tests.

STEPS TO A POSITIVE ATTITUDE

The following will help you be positive about your ability and to aggressively attack tests.

Principle 2.11: Practice for the test.

If you practice answering questions like the ones that will be on the test, this will increase your confidence. By checking your answers, you will also be able to judge how well you know the material. If you are consistently answering your study questions correctly, you can believe that you will also answer test questions correctly.

Principle 2.12: Find out as much as you can about the test.

One reason people worry is fear of the unknown. If you can find out about your test and specifically prepare for it, there is no need to worry about the unknown. Of course, you will never know the exact questions. But if you study and practice a wide range of questions that are like questions to be on your test, you should feel very confident.

Principle 2.13: Make sure you understand the test directions.

Many students have panicked when they first saw a test because they did not understand the directions. If test directions seem unclear or confusing, ask for help from your teacher. It is always better to ask than to just sit and worry and waste valuable test time.

Principle 2.14: Relax before the test.

Get to the test room early to avoid rushing, but not so early that you have to wait a long time. Find a comfortable place to sit, and just relax until you are given the test. You may want to do a last-minute check of some memorized facts, but, other than this, be confident in your study. Tense and then relax each of your body muscles, and take a few deep breaths.

Principle 2.15: Force worry out of your mind.

If you find you are worrying, you can do two things: (1) Tell yourself you do not need to worry, you are probably the best prepared student in the class. (2) Think about something else that is pleasant, such as a social date or hobby. Do not let yourself get caught in a worry trap, which could affect your test grade.

Principle 2.16: Use luck to your advantage.

We all feel better about ourselves sometimes than other times. These positive feelings can be associated with certain clothes, seat location, type of pen or pencil, or many other things. We often believe these things bring us good luck. If you have some lucky items, be sure to take them to the test with you. No one knows why, but these things help us be more confident.

Principle 2.17: Do not wait until the last minute to prepare for a test.

Most students who study for a test all night and only the night before the test are nervous. They have every right to worry. They are tired, probably hungry, know very little, have essentially no practice, and have little chance of remembering much. This kind of preparation promotes worry and anxiety. You are at your best when you are rested, relaxed, and confident. This condition is difficult to achieve if you've been up all night in a panic studying for the test.

SUMMARY

The purpose of this chapter has been to help you prepare to take tests. First, find out as much as you can about the test. Then use a variety of study skills to prepare yourself to take the test. These study skills allow you to control and manage your studying in order to learn, understand, and get good test grades.

Seven study skill principles will help you become actively involved, understand what you study, relate new material to what you already know, maintain interest, and test yourself—the characteristics of good students. Specifically, these principles are:

Principle 2.2: Set study goals.
Principle 2.3: Survey first.
Principle 2.4: Prepare study questions.
Principle 2.5: Plan your study time.
Principle 2.6: Read for main ideas.
Principle 2.7: Regularly test your confidence.
Principle 2.8: Solidify your learning by summarizing.

Each of these principles includes several specific actions for increasing test scores. If you are not learning using one action, you have many others to use.

The following are principles for improving your memory:

Principle 2.9: Organize the information you must remember.
Principle 2.10: Use memory techniques or tricks.

Like study skills, you can control what you remember by using these techniques.

Teachers have different expectations of students. Knowing the three types of learning expectations makes it possible to focus study.

Finally, a good attitude toward tests is important. For an aggressive and confident test taker, a test is an opportunity to demonstrate what has been learned. Confidence can be increased by following these principles:

Principle 2.11: Practice for the test.
Principle 2.12: Find out as much as you can about the test.
Principle 2.13: Make sure you understand test directions.
Principle 2.14: Relax before the test.
Principle 2.15: Force worry out of your mind.
Principle 2.16: Use luck to your advantage.
Principle 2.17: Do not wait until the last minute to prepare for a test.

Good study uses time in better ways by using better study skills. The result is better test scores.

Action Practice

Here are some practice exercises to help you use the principles in chapter 2.

1. Think of your next test and write the answers to the following questions.
   a. What day is the test? What time? Where?
   b. What kind of questions will be on the test?
   c. What type of learning will your professor expect you to demonstrate?
   d. What pages in your textbook will the test cover?
   e. Which class lectures will the test cover?
   f. What specific topics will be on the test?
   g. Will you get one of the highest scores on the test?
   If you cannot answer all of these questions, you do not know enough about your next test.

2. Read the following passage actively:

   Anyone can become a good test taker. All that is required is a little effort and belief in yourself that you can succeed. We have seen many students who feared and dreaded taking tests learn to actually look forward to their next test. This change was the result of these students learning how to study and how to take tests.

   What is involved in learning to look forward to taking tests? The first thing is to consider tests as opportunities to demonstrate what you know. You cannot view yourself as stupid and your professor as interested in seeing just how stupid you are. On the contrary, you must see yourself as an able and prepared student who knows a lot. You must attack tests with relish and enthusiasm. You must want to let out, as it were, all the knowledge inside you. You must want to show you can do it; you can be a good student.

Anyone can develop such an attitude with a little effort because all of us can control what we learn. We can study aggressively by attacking new information as an opportunity to improve our understanding. We can develop a variety of learning skills that we can use to help us learn even very difficult information. Using a single learning skill is unsuccessful. It is surprising how many students have only one way of studying. Even when they are unsuccessful, some students continue to use just one strategy. They do not seem to realize that not understanding is a clue that another learning skill is needed. Sometimes, these students think not understanding right away is an indication that they are incapable.

Too many students do not realize that they can learn to take tests. Taking tests is like other skill areas; if you understand how to take tests, you are bound to do better. Think about trying to fly an airplane. If you have never been in the cockpit of an airplane, you would not have the slightest idea of what to do. But you can learn what all the knobs and switches and dials on an airplane are for and learn to fly. It is the same for taking tests.

Even though most of us have taken lots of tests, most of us do not know why teachers choose to give a certain kind of test. Even worse, many students do not know they can learn to take tests by learning about the special characteristics of tests. Let us assure you, if you are willing to learn about tests and believe in yourself, you can get good test grades.

The main problem with any test is to figure out how you can demonstrate what you know. Just knowing something is not enough in school: You also must know how to demonstrate what you know. Knowing how to take tests helps you learn to demonstrate what you know.

Now, check yourself for active reading.
a. Did you survey the passage before you read? You could have surveyed the passage by reading the first sentence in each paragraph. Or you could have read the first and last paragraphs.
b. Did you ask yourself any questions? You could have begun by asking yourself, "What is this about?" After reading only the first paragraph, you could have asked, "What did these students do to learn to look forward to tests?"

You could also have asked yourself, "Do I look forward to taking tests?" "Why not?" "What can I find out that will help me look forward to taking tests?"
c. The passage has no title. Can you supply a title? If you can, this probably means you understood the passage. Some good titles might be: "You Can Become a Good Test Taker," "The Impor-

tance of Demonstrating What You Know," and "Developing the Ability to Take Tests."

d. What do you think is the purpose of this passage? Why did the author write this passage? If you cannot answer these questions, you may have missed the point because you were not reading actively. The passage was written to convince you that anyone can become a good test taker by studying effectively and learning how to take tests.

e. Summarize the main point of the passage in your own words. Check your answer by reviewing the passage and seeing if you are accurate.

3. Now, practice improving your memory.

a. If you had to remember the following words, how would you do it?

Car, light bulb, match, tape, train, glue, motorcycle, star, rail, airplane

The list is hard to remember because it appears to be a list of random words. Remember that organization is the key to good memory, so look for some organization. There are three kinds of words in this list: transportation words, words that hold things together, and words that are related to light. Having these three organizational categories makes remembering the list of words easier.

b. Every airplane pilot has to remember to do four things before landing a plane. They have to check that they are using the proper gas tank; they have to lower the landing gear on the undercarriage; they must set the fuel mixture properly; and they have to set the pitch of the propeller.

Can you construct an acronym to help pilots remember all this information? Before reading further, develop an acronym.

Pilots use the acronym GUMP to help remember all they must do before landing. G = gas; U = undercarriage, M = mixture, and P = propeller.

c. Develop an acronym to help you remember the seven principles on study skills. You may recall the rhyme we presented to help remember these principles.

Goals, Survey, Quest

Plan, Ideas, Test

and Summarize

Try an acronym before reading further. The best acronyms are ones you make up yourself.

Here is one we made up: Go Serve Q PITS. To make the acronym even better as a memory aid, we also visualize an image of a waiter serving an angry teacher named Quigly a plate of peach pits for dinner. Go = goals; $Serve$ = survey; Q = question; P = plan; I = read for main ideas; and S = summarize.

If any of these action practice exercises was difficult for you, do not be discouraged. They are difficult for most people who have not tried them. If these exercises were difficult, it means you need to practice. With practice you can learn to use all of the skills described in this chapter.

Multiple-Choice Tests

Being able to take multiple-choice tests is one of the most important things you can do to make better grades. The multiple-choice test is an extremely popular kind of test in education, as well as in business and industry. Your task with multiple-choice questions seems rather simple. You are given either a question or incomplete statement and then must select one correct answer from several choices. Yet, despite this apparent simplicity, most of us know that multiple-choice tests can be very demanding. Consistently good performance requires both skill and an aggressive attitude.

In this chapter, we will present the information you need to make yourself a skilled and aggressive multiple-choice-test taker. We begin by describing the characteristics of multiple-choice tests so you can understand why many instructors like to use them. This is followed by certain principles that describe what to do while taking a multiple-choice test. These principles are designed to help you avoid mistakes, use your knowledge well, and improve your test scores. Finally, we will give some suggestions to help you study for a multiple-choice test.

CHARACTERISTICS OF MULTIPLE-CHOICE TESTS

The multiple-choice test is probably the most popular and widely used test form. For most multiple-choice tests, questions will look like this:

Stem	When the volume of a given mass of gas is kept constant, the pressure may be increased by
Options or Alternatives	1. reducing the temperature 2. raising the temperature 3. decreasing density 4. increasing density

The first statement or question is called the stem. The stem is followed by several possible answers, only one of which is correct. In this chapter, we will refer to these several possible answers as *alternatives* or *options*. The correct answer is the alternative that best completes the statement or answers the question presented in the stem. The incorrect options, the ones you try not to select, are called distractors. Writers of test questions usually try to prepare distractors that all look equally attractive to you if you do not know the material. Thus, when prepared by an expert writer, multiple-choice questions can be very difficult.

Multiple-choice questions are popular for at least two reasons. For one thing, the multiple-choice format gives your teacher a great deal of flexibility in making up a test. Because it normally takes only a brief amount of time to respond to any one question, a lot of material can be covered on a single test. Also, multiple-choice questions can be used to measure performance on several different types of learning. In fact, it is possible to measure each type of learning described in Chapter 2 (see Table 1.1 in Chapter 2). However, most teachers seem to emphasize how much information (Type I learning) you know. In the following examples, notice that questions *can* differ a great deal depending on the type of learning the instructor wants you to demonstrate:

Verbatim Recall Question (Type I)

The Monroe Doctrine was announced about ten years after the
1. Revolutionary War
2. War of 1812
3. Civil War
4. Spanish-American War

Comprehension Type Question (Type II)

An investigator noted spotted coats in a population of wild house mice. He bred two spotted mice repeatedly and obtained 100 offsprings—all spotted. The best interpretation is that the trait is
1. a blend
2. dominant
3. inherited
4. recessive
5. sex-linked

Analysis Type Question (Type II)

Which of the following statements best describes the author's conclusion?
1. Voluntary fuel rationing is unlikely.
2. Any fuel rationing is bad.
3. Mandatory fuel rationing is unnecessary.
4. Mandatory fuel rationing is bad.
5. Mandatory fuel rationing is impossible.

Clearly, these three questions require different levels of ability. The factual question can be answered by recalling a single fact concerning the timing of the Monroe Doctrine. The second question, however, requires use of several facts and concepts to interpret the meaning of the biologist's findings. This question cannot be solved simply by recalling verbatim some fact. Finally, the third question requires students to identify one particular element, the conclusion, of a given passage. In this case, the passage must be analyzed to determine which conclusion was implied by the author.

The primary limitation of multiple-choice questions is that they are very difficult to write. A good question could require from one to three hours to prepare. Few instructors can invest this much time in classroom tests. Consequently most of the tests you take (excluding the major standardized tests) will have some flaws. Later in this chapter, we will describe some of the typical mistakes in multiple-choice tests and show how to use them to improve your test scores. While there is no substitute for having a lot of knowledge and knowing how to use it, having the combination of both knowledge and test-taking skill is an unbeatable combination.

TAKING MULTIPLE-CHOICE TESTS

There are several action principles that will help you take multiple-choice tests. We have divided this information into the following four categories:

1. Use smart general test-taking tactics. These are actions successful test takers employ on *all* tests.

2. Know the specific characteristics of multiple-choice tests. These characteristics can help you figure out the answer; this is particularly important when you know something about the material, but are not really sure of the answer.

3. Exercise logical skills to reason out the correct answer when several alternatives look reasonable. These are skills that all people have, but very few practice consistently.

4. Finally, learn to pick up clues to correct answers, which can be found in the questions themselves. In many teacher-made tests, it is amazing how often the answer to some questions can be correctly selected by using cues in the test.

USING GOOD TEST-TAKING TACTICS

Principle 3.1: Budget your time.

One reason teachers like multiple-choice tests is that a great deal of material can be covered on a single test. As a result, multiple-choice tests usually contain many questions that will have to be answered in a short period of time. You should begin each test by checking its length and estimating how much time is available for each item. Many times, you will find that 60 or more questions need to be covered in a single hour. This means that you have a minute or less to respond to each question! This may seem impossible in some cases, but remember, many questions will require only a few seconds. Consider the following questions:

> A chemical change is demonstrated by
> 1. wax melting
> 2. oil burning
> 3. alcohol evaporating
> 4. water freezing

> Which of the following is a kilocalorie?
> 1. a unit of energy
> 2. one kilogram of water at 1°C
> 3. a unit of temperature
> 4. one pound of water at 1°F

These questions require factual recall, and, even if you are not completely sure of the material, an answer for each can be selected in ten or fifteen seconds. If you work at a reasonable pace through a multiple-choice test, there should be enough time to spare for tougher questions.

Principle 3.2: Keep moving at a steady pace through the test. Come back to difficult questions that you could not solve initially.

Read through and answer *all* questions you know first, and skip the ones you are not sure of. Most of the questions you *can* answer will take very little time. Then recalculate your time so you know how much to spend on each remaining question. Do not spend more than the alloted time, and, again, skip those you cannot figure out. Then calculate time again, and reread each unanswered question. Never rush, but work within your time schedule. If you manage your time, you will not have to rush and can work confidently.

We have seen tests in which instructors included more questions than could be reasonably answered in the time given. Be aware that you should devote at least some set amount of time to each question. For example, you should plan to spend fifteen to twenty seconds on each item (no more than three to four questions per minute). If you can work faster, that is fine; but set a realistic maximum time for each question, and stick to it. You can come back to the questions you do not know after you answer all the questions you *do* know.

Principle 3.3.: Respond to the test according to directions.

We have seen many students begin tests without even glancing at the directions. One common direction included in multiple-choice tests is to select the *best* alternative for each question. This is sometimes different from your usual understanding that there is only a single correct alternative. It will help you to know that for many questions on multiple-choice tests more than one alternative may have degrees of correctness, but that only one is considered best. What happens in many cases is that a student reads the stem of the question, immediately sees a "good" or "attractive" alternative, and then selects that alternative without examining the remaining choices. It is possible to miss an obviously correct and better alternative simply because you failed to even read it in your haste to select the first good alternative. Therefore, *always read every alternative!* In a well-prepared question, all the alternatives could look attractive; however, only *one* will be graded as correct.

Consider the following two examples that are similar to items being used in pilot training programs:

Which procedure is recommended to prevent or overcome vertigo?
1. Use a combination of feel and sight.
2. Avoid steep turns and rough control movements.
3. Rely entirely upon the indications of the flight instruments.
4. Use a very rapid cross-check.

How can a pilot best overcome vertigo?
1. Avoid turns of more than 30°
2. Use supplemental oxygen.
3. Use a very rapid cross-check.
4. Rely on the sense of sight.

In each of these questions, there is more than one alternative that has some degree of correctness. However, we are told that for all questions dealing with vertigo, the *best* alternative will call for reliance on the sense of sight *only*.

Thus, the best answers are number 3 and number 4, respectively, for the first and second examples above.

Directions are also used to give other valuable information, such as how to mark answers, what the time limits are, whether there is a penalty for guessing, whether you can make notes on the test booklet and/or answer sheet, how answers will be scored, and so forth.

Principle 3.4: Find out in advance what the test will require of you.

Avoid surprises on tests. Generally, you will be able to obtain lots of information by being alert in class. Note the key points made by the instructor, and try to determine whether you are going to have to remember facts or whether more complex learning, such as analysis and problem solving, will be required.

One good strategy is to ask to see examples of previous tests or examples of questions the instructor has given. If these are not available, ask the instructor to make a key point into a typical question. In fact, ask for several examples. Very few students ask to see actual test questions, although in most cases professors would be willing to share a few examples.

Another aid is to make a list of things you know the instructor will question you about. Sometimes your instructor will tell you; sometimes you just know because the point is repeated so many times. In any event, you should construct answers to those questions well in advance of the test. Knowing what to expect is a tremendous advantage. It saves you time in both studying and test taking and will give additional confidence. Students who know what to expect will be much less anxious on test day.

Principle 3.5: Aggressively attack the test with the idea that each question can be answered.

On tough tests, each problem can be a struggle. Be prepared to use all the knowledge you have. Multiple-choice questions can be used to help you remember much of what you have studied. Because you do not actually have to construct an answer, you can use both the question stems and alternatives as cues to help you remember course material. Aggressive test takers rely on what they know to ''figure out'' which alternative is correct. Remember, you may not be able to recognize the correct response immediately. Sometimes, at first glance, they all look equally good. In fact, your instructor intends for each alternative to look equally good to those who do not know the material.

Here are two examples that demonstrate what we mean by figuring out an answer:

Increasing the length of a test would most likely increase its
1. complexity
2. difficulty
3. reliability
4. validity

Lift produced by an airfoil is the net force developed perpendicular to the
1. earth's surface
2. relative wind
3. chord
4. longitudinal axis of the aircraft

At first glance, it may be very difficult to determine which answer is correct for either of these questions. In the first example, the good test taker would consider each of the options, trying to think how length (number of items on a test) would fit into each concept. Only reliability (number 3) contains test length as a part of its formula. In the second example, it may be useful for the test taker to remember pictures and other demonstrations of the lift concept. In doing so, it may be possible to reconstruct from memory the correct answer, relative wind (number 2).

RESPONDING TO MULTIPLE-CHOICE TESTS

Here is what the average instructor does when preparing a test question. First, a small piece of content is selected, and a stem is written. The stem is the first part that you encounter, and it is used to specify the task the instructor wants you to perform. These tasks vary, of course, but the following two examples represent the most common types of stems:

Posing an Incomplete Sentence
The stages in the life of a housefly are, in order . . .
During the process of normal breathing . . .
Scientists discover new facts by . . .
The immediate causes of unconsciousness were probably . . .

Asking a Direct Question
Which of the following is not a chemical change?
Which of the following is the best example of a behaviorally written objective?
Which of the following is the best description of the article as a whole?
Which of the following assumptions was violated in the statistical analysis?

The instructor must then *generate*, or make up, four or five plausible alternatives for each question or incomplete sentence. To be sure, both the stem and the correct alternative (the answer) could be copied almost directly from text material. However, this still leaves three or four good alternatives yet to be written. Unless this instructor is an expert in test construction, at least some of the alternatives will be easily identifiable as incorrect solutions to the task posed in the stem. Some may even be outright absurd or silly.

Principle 3.6: If the correct answer is not immediately obvious, eliminate alternatives that are obviously absurd, silly, or incorrect.

The key here is to improve your chances by changing the question from a four- or five-choice task to a two- or three-choice task. You can usually do this on most tests constructed by nonprofessional test writers. To the extent that you eliminate alternatives, you are making the test easier. Read the following test question, and try to determine whether one or more of the alternatives can be eliminated simply because they are not serious contenders.

When attempting to solve a problem, a scientist's first step is usually to
1. guess at the answers
2. purchase equipment
3. gather all available information on the subject
4. draw conclusions
5. perform an experiment

Some of these alternatives would not make sense to anyone even remotely acquainted with scientific methodology. Alternatives 1 and 4 are clearly absurd as first steps, so these can be eliminated immediately. However, alternatives 2 and 5 may be steps required at some time during the scientist's problem-solving process, but probably will not be done first. This question can be quickly reduced by most people to choosing among three choices. For those who have some knowledge, two of the remaining alternatives may be eliminated, leaving only the correct answer (number 3).

Here is another example:

Which of the following has the greatest momentum?
1. a thrown baseball
2. a jet aircraft in flight
3. a jet aircraft taxiing toward the ramp
4. a parked jet aircraft

On this question, students with only a little knowledge about momentum may be able to use information about size and speed to identify the correct response (number 2). However, if one knows only that momentum is related to movement, then alternative 4 can be dismissed as very unlikely. This means that if you have to guess, you are now responding to an easier problem. This leads us to the next principle.

Principle 3.7: Always guess if you do not know the answer.

Now, here is how principles 3.6 and 3.7 work together. Each alternative you eliminate improves the probability of guessing the correct response. The figures below show the mathematical probabilities of guessing the correct answer with different numbers of alternatives.

Number of Alternatives	Probability of Guessing the Correct Answer
5 choices	.20
4 choices	.25
3 choices	.33
2 choices	.50
1 choice	1.00

As you can see, the probability of guessing the correct answer improves considerably if you can eliminate some of the alternatives. Here is how the process might work when five-choice items are used. Let us assume that on a sixty-item test you know for sure only thirty responses. Your score at this point is 30. Now, if you blindly guess on the remaining thirty, you can expect to obtain, on the average, six additional points. Your score is now a 36. Suppose, however, that you could successfully eliminate all but two alternatives on each of the thirty items you did not know. You could now expect to obtain 15 additional points by guessing. This gives you a score of 45, which is often a respectable showing on sixty-item multiple-choice tests. Therefore, it pays to guess. Now, we will examine further some methods you can use to reduce or eliminate alternatives.

Principle 3.8: Compare each alternative to the stem and to other alternatives.

The correct answer must effectively answer the questions or complete the sentence presented in the stem of the question. There are several things you can do to compare the stem with alternatives.

Do not make the question more difficult than it really is. When you do not know the answer for sure, it is tempting to change a word or two, either in the stem or in one or more alternatives, to make the question look like one to which you can respond. Keep the instructor's perspective in mind, and always answer the question as written.

Relate each remaining option to the stem. Sometimes, alternatives will look attractive by themselves. However, the correct alternative must fit with the stem even if it does not look like the best statement when considered alone. Consider the following question, which we have found to cause problems for students who do not relate the alternative to the stem:

> Which of the following is the best behavioral objective?
> 1. The student will indicate knowledge of 17th-century art and the people who contributed during that time.
> 2. The student will select examples of inductive reasoning from descriptions of scientific procedures.
> 3. The student will be able to know the thirteen amendments to the Constitution with 80 percent accuracy.
> 4. The student will develop skills in interpersonal relationships through small, informal, honest, and meaningful exchanges with the peer group.

In this example, the correct answer is number 2 because it specifies most clearly the exact behavior required of the student. The student activities described in the remaining three options do not meet as well the accepted rule that instructional objectives specify observable and measurable behaviors. However, in this question we find that a large proportion of students select option 3 because, by itself, it appears to represent the most complete objective, since it also contains information about the criteria (80 percent accuracy) the student must meet. In short, alternative number 3 is attractive by itself, even though it does not directly answer the question. Likewise, alternative number 4 also "looks good," probably because of the number of qualifiers used to describe "exchanges with the peer group." We find that many students who select the incorrect alternatives, 3 and 4, will eventually agree that option 2 is a better answer to the question. However, many still find it difficult to completely forget alternatives that by themselves "feel" correct or look better. Do not fall into this trap! Select the one alternative that best answers the question in the stem. Here is an example:

> As an essayist and thinker, James Fenimore Cooper produced some interesting criticism of American democracy. Which of the following was *not* one of Cooper's beliefs about democracy?
> 1. The success of a democracy depends primarily on the intelligence of people.
> 2. Small democracies are more practical than large ones.
> 3. Democracies are controlled by public opinion.
> 4. Democracies are the least expensive form of government.

In this case, the trick is to examine each option and then ask, "Is this *not* one of Cooper's beliefs about democracy?" Number 2 is the option that does not fit.

Relate each remaining option to the other remaining options.
Directly compare alternatives and analyze how they are different. Focus directly on key points that make one correct and the other incorrect. Consider the following example:

> The relationship between density and pressure of gasses shown in Boyle's law, P = KD, remains true
> 1. for some gasses under all conditions
> 2. for all gasses under all conditions
> 3. only if the density is constant
> 4. only if the temperature is held constant

Here the conditions under which Boyle's simple law of gasses will hold true must be understood. Examination of each of the alternatives reveals two options specifying that the law holds under all conditions and two specifying that the law is true only under a specific condition. Even with only partial knowledge, many students will correctly decide to reject any proposition stating that the law holds under "all conditions." This leaves two options, one that density must be held constant and the other that temperature must be held constant. Since density is already mentioned in the formula, it makes sense to suspect that a third variable might be involved. A good choice is to select option 4, which is the correct response. This kind of thinking would be even easier if one had some knowledge that temperature does affect the pressure of gasses. Consider another example:

> Which of the following scores appearing in a permanent record would be most meaningful without further reference to the entire group?
> 1. 32 items correct in an English test of 40 items
> 2. 30 items wrong in an Algebra test of 70 items
> 3. 100 words per minute on a typewriting test
> 4. 20 errors on a test of shorthand

By comparing each option, the test taker should be able to see that one item has something all the others do not. In this question, what is needed is a score that can be readily interpreted without any additional information. Option 3 is the only one meeting that criteria.

In summary, because multiple-choice tests are difficult to make up, not all alternatives will be equally good. As a result, some alternatives may be eliminated, thus improving your chances if guessing becomes necessary. Your goal is to use your existing knowledge to eliminate wrong alternatives and to find the correct option. The best way to do this is to consider each alternative carefully and relate each to the stem and to each other. Do not guess wildly or select an alternative that simply looks and reads attractively.

USING LOGICAL REASONING TO IMPROVE PERFORMANCE

When unsure about an answer, many students will correctly eliminate the obviously wrong "give-away" options and then blindly guess among the remaining alternatives. You can do better than this by using your logical reasoning skills. Because we often rely too much on rote memory, we forget that we can reconstruct answers through careful thinking. In this section, we will help you apply logical reasoning to successful test taking.

Principle 3.9: Whenever two or more options are identical, then both must be incorrect.

In order to obtain the desired number of alternatives, a teacher will sometimes duplicate an existing alternative by stating it differently. Consider the following example:

> At the present rate of use, fossil fuels
> 1. will be adequate for thousands of years
> 2. are essentially inexhaustible
> 3. will at best last only a few generations more
> 4. will never be totally expended

Since there is only one correct answer, alternatives 2 and 4 may be eliminated outright, since they are identical statements. This leaves only two options, which gives you a 50-50 chance if you guess. However, many of you would be able to recognize number 3 as the correct answer, based on even marginal information. Try one more example:

> In a family of nine sons and two daughters, the chances that the next child will be a daughter are:
> 1. $^2/_9$
> 2. $^1/_9$
> 3. $^4/_{18}$
> 4. $^1/_2$

In this example, two options (1 and 3) can be eliminated outright because they are identical. The correct answer is alternative 4.

Principle 3.10: If any two options are opposites, then at least one may be eliminated.

If one option is correct, then the other must be incorrect. Of course, both may be incorrect, leaving some third option as the correct choice. Consider the following example:

Which of the following arguments did Copernicus use in favor of his system?
1. It was consistent with good common sense.
2. It was in keeping with Christian beliefs.
3. It was more accurate than any existing system.
4. It did not hold with Christian beliefs.

Look at alternatives 2 and 4; at least one has to be incorrect. This does not give away the answer, but every clue helps when the answer is not known for sure. Frequently, when two alternatives contradict each other, as in this example, one of the two will be correct. An easy procedure for professors to use in developing alternatives is to include the reverse of the correct answer. Thus, examine opposites carefully, they may contain more information than you think.

Principle 3.11: Choose the alternative that is most inclusive.

Here is an example:

Which of the following influences contributed to the conflict between Philip II and Elizabeth I?
1. religion
2. politics
3. a combination of religion and politics
4. trade conflicts
5. the true cause has never been firmly established

In this case, options 1 and 2 are both correct. However, since option 3 includes both of these two correct statements, then it should be keyed as the correct response. The principle of selecting the most inclusive alternative is also valuable in dealing with questions that have ''all of the above'' and ''none of the above'' as options. Often, these kinds of options are used to effectively combine a lot of information to produce a correct answer.

Another logical skill that can be helpful in multiple-choice tests is to look for the answer to questions in the stems of other items. Sometimes cues or outright answers are given in other questions included in the test. This is another reason for reading all the questions before attempting to answer ones you do not know.

Here is an example of an answer to one question appearing in another question:

> Which of the following is the best example of an operant?
> 1. talking
> 2. a behavioral contract
> 3. receiving praise
> 4. relaxing
>
> Such operant behaviors as talking or writing are more powerfully influenced when
> 1. reinforcement is delayed
> 2. reinforcement is immediate
> 3. reinforcement is not used
> 4. reinforcement is self-administered

A clue to answering the first item is found in the stem of the second, which tells you that talking and writing are operant behaviors. Cues like this are often found in multiple-choice tests.

USING CLUES IN THE TEST

Principle 3.12: Use test flaws to help you guess.

Psychologists who study multiple-choice tests have identified nine errors commonly made by instructors writing such tests. Instructors are encouraged to avoid these errors because they ''give away'' the correct answer. If you see any of these errors, they may help you choose the correct answer. You should always rely most on your knowledge. But if you have to guess, these common errors will help you be a better guesser:

Length. Whenever you need to choose among alternatives that look equally attractive, select the longer one. Longer options are more frequently correct because they contain elaborations or qualifications needed to make that option clearly correct. This is true of the following question:

> The pilot in command of a civil aircraft must have an instrument rating *only* when operating
> 1. under instrument flight rules, in weather conditions less than the minimum prescribed for VFR flight, and in a positive control area or route segment

2. in controlled airspace in weather conditions less than the minimum prescribed for VFR flight
3. in controlled airspace when operating under instrument flight rules
4. in weather conditions less than the minimum prescribed for VFR flight

In this case, the longer answer (number 1) was necessary to cover all conditions specified in the rule referred to in the stem.

Location. The correct answer will be found more often in middle positions than in extreme (first or last) locations. Teachers usually will write one or two distractors, place the correct answer next, and then finish with one or two additional distractors. This is true of the next example, in which 3 is the correct answer.

What type of clouds will be formed if very stable moist air is forced upslope?
1. vertical clouds with increasing height
2. layer-like clouds with little vertical development
3. first, layer clouds and then vertical clouds
4. first, vertical clouds and then layer clouds

Grammar. Look for alternatives that do not match the stem gramatically. The stem and the correct response usually will be written as a single, grammatically correct unit. Incorrect alternatives may not be prepared with such care. Here is an example:

Each of the twelve poems discussed depends on a _____ for its effect.
1. cliché
2. metaphor
3. imagery
4. allusion

In this case, only options 1 and 2 could fit correctly into the stem. Options 3 and 4 should thus be discarded.

Language. Unusual or overly technical language usually indicates an incorrect alternative. Even those only slightly familiar with the content should be able to recognize and avoid alternatives that include unusual terminology.

Familiar or verbatim phrases. The easiest way to construct a question is to take one directly from text or from lectures. Therefore, it is good advice to select a stem-option combination that looks most familiar. In the following example, the definition of *imprinting* was taken verbatim from text material:

Learning that only occurs during a critical period is called
1. critical conditioning
2. respondent conditioning
3. encoding
4. imprinting

Qualified answers. Frequently, the correct option will contain qualifiers—such words or phrases as *in most cases, as reported in, generally, frequently, except when.* Here is an example in which the correct option (2) contains the qualifier *tend to be*:

In general, females
1. do not concentrate on obtaining good grades as hard as males do
2. tend to be more compliant toward the academic expectations of the school
3. perform poorer overall in high school when compared with males
4. do not become involved in educational endeavors that have low interest values

Generalized reponses. Correct options will also tend to have wider applicability or be more flexible than the incorrect, less general options. In the next example, option 3 gives the appropriately flexible (and correct) response.

During the summer, without additional instruction, students' achievement
1. decreases
2. increases
3. may either increase or decrease depending upon the subject

Specific determiners. *Never, always,* and similar words are usually not included in the correct response. In most cases, these words make the response too narrow or restricted to be correct. This is true of options 2 and 3 below. In this case, option 4 is correct.

Harlow's findings show that
1. absence of a real mother figure did not hamper the infant monkey's social and emotional maturation
2. "cloth" mothers played no role in reducing the infant monkey's fear in anxiety-provoking situations
3. satisfaction of the hunger drive singly promotes and nurtures the infant's attachment for the mother
4. attachment for the mother is promoted by the need to establish contact with something that can offer comfort and warmth

STUDYING FOR MULTIPLE-CHOICE TESTS

With multiple-choice tests, you do not have to construct a response or provide specific details to support your answers. Multiple-choice tests obviously do not require composition ability, organizational skills, and spelling skills to effectively show what you know. In this sense, such tests present an easier task than do other kinds of tests, such as essay tests.

On the other hand, multiple-choice tests are capable of covering a very broad range of material during a normal testing period. Moreover, the material may be covered in considerable detail. To get a good test grade, you must effectively organize and use a relatively large amount of information. To be ready to answer the questions presented by the instructor, you must thoroughly study all assigned material, predict what topics are most important, and use good study skills.

Do not rely solely on your own intuition and class notes to decide what to study. Ask the professor to describe or identify the material to be covered on the test. Find out what kind of questions are likely to be on the test. If old tests are available (ask the professor, ask students who have taken the course previously, consult fraternity/sorority files, etc.), these will be your best sources of direct information about a particular instructor's tests. If all these sources fail, then at least ask the professor to give several examples of typical questions. This will give you a hint of the intellectual level of the test.

Perhaps most important, do not focus on details to the extent that you lose sight of the big picture. Our discussion in Chapter 2, dealing with constructing summaries and outlines, made this point.

Let us trace your steps through your next multiple-choice test. We shall begin by assuming that you have accomplished the following:

- You have generally determined what the test will cover, including both content and type of learning to be demonstrated.
- You have prepared for the test by using the techniques described in Chapter 2. Your focus has been on understanding, rather than on rote recall.
- You have reviewed briefly just before the exam by reading over your own personally organized summary and notes.

Arriving at the test, you experience a little tension, but recognize that this will help you to attack the test aggressively. You relax your body and feel confident about your ability to do well on the test. After receiving the test, you

- Put everything out of your mind except the task at hand—solving each of the test questions.

- Listen to any verbal directions and carefully read all written directions before attempting to answer any test question.
- Ask questions immediately if any of the directions are unclear.
- Look over the test quickly and decide how to budget your time.
- Read and answer each question in turn; skip only questions that are too difficult or for which you run out of allotted time.
- Attack all questions, regardless of difficulty, as opportunities to demonstrate what you know and to test your test-taking skills.
- For each question, read and consider *every* alternative.
- Eliminate immediately any absurd or silly alternatives.
- To decide among alternatives that remain attractive to you, use all available strategies—compare alternatives, use logic to detect which alternatives to retain or reject.
- Look for cues to locate correct options when all else fails.
- If still undecided among two or more alternatives, always guess instead of leaving the item blank.
- After finishing all questions, go back to rethink any you could not solve at first. On especially tough problems, check to see whether any other questions may give you a clue.
- Check to see that you did not make any errors on the answer sheet.

SUMMARY

The multiple-choice test is popular because a lot of content can be covered and a variety of types of learning may be tested. Good performance requires knowledge of all the content covered on the test. To use this information well, treat each question as a problem that can be solved by knowing the answer outright, by carefully comparing two or more options, by logically deducing the correct answer, by making an informed guess, or by using cues in the test. Of course, all of these strategies may be used together.

Action Practice

In this chapter, we have given twelve action principles designed to help you improve your score on multiple-choice tests. These principles can help you beginning with the very next test you take. However, to ensure the greatest success, you should plan to practice these skills whenever you can. Consciously apply the principles and observe the effects of your efforts on every test you take.

Here are a few practice questions to get you started. Mark the *best* answer on each item. Your score will be the number of correct answers.

1. Weight can best be defined as
   a. the force with which a body is attracted to the earth by gravitational forces
   b. mass of an object
   c. density of an object
   d. a standard

2. Which of these equations is correct?
   a. $3g + 7 = 10 + 6g$, where $g = 1$
   b. $10 + 6n = 25 + 4n$, where $n = 1\frac{1}{2}$
   c. $12n - 8 = -15 + 10n$, where $n = 2\frac{1}{2}$
   d. $10 + 6z = 3z + 7$, where $z = 1$

3. A *sect* is best defined as
   a. a group adhering to a particular doctrine
   b. a religious body
   c. a secret organization
   d. a political structure

4. Since 1950, the trend in urban transportation has been toward greater use of
   a. trains
   b. autos
   c. rickshaws
   d. motorcycles

5. The normal boiling temperature of a liquid is
   a. 212°F
   b. 100°C
   c. that point at which it emits steam
   d. the temperature at which the vapor pressure of that liquid is exactly one standard atmosphere.

6. The hearing-impaired child's achievement is
   a. always below grade level
   b. comparable to the hearing population
   c. generally somewhat below average
   d. very likely above average

7. In the computer language PL/1, a legitimate line delimiter is a
   a. not needed
   b. semicolon
   c. colons
   d. vertical bars

8. Handling sodium hydroxide with moist hands
   a. is not dangerous
   b. will result in severe damage
   c. may result in severe burns
   d. produces a marked hydroxemic rash

9. If you wish to use solubility to help in identifying a substance, you need a
   a. evaluative assessment of conductivity
   b. solubility index
   c. test of the substance's molecular structure
   d. quantitative measure to compare with a table of known solubilities

10. The term *fauvism* refers to
    a. a vibrant and decorative artistic effect
    b. a mistake
    c. a gentle and subdued effect
    d. a statement of positive regard

Answers

1. This question poses a relatively easy problem that is made even simpler if you use the cue provided by the relative *length* of alternative *a*. If you are not sure of the correct answer, you can often rely on the generalization that the longer options are more likely to be correct. Option *a* is correct in this case.

2. The careful reader will notice that options *a* and *d* are identical and thus must be eliminated as explained in Principle 3.9. This leaves only two options—a little arithmetic will show that option *b* is correct.

3. The correct answer is *a* because it is the most inclusive answer (see Principle 3.11). Each of the remaining options describes a *particular* type of sect and thus does not qualify as the best definition.

4. Alternative *c* in question 4 should be eliminated outright as an absurd choice (see Principle 3.6), which leaves you with a somewhat easier three-choice problem. You probably identified *b* as the correct choice after comparing the three remaining options with the stem (Principle 3.8).

5. The correct answer for question 5 is *d*. Options *a* and *b* are identical and must be eliminated (see Principle 3.9). Further, the length of the *d* option gives an additional cue as to its correctness.

6. Several options contain qualifiers. Generally, you should avoid options with universal qualifiers (*a*) in favor of those with relative qualifiers (*c*). Option *c* is the correct answer.

7. Grammar problems (lack of subject-verb agreement) in question 7 allow you to discard options *a, c,* and *d.* Alternative *b* is the correct choice.

8. Qualifiers are again used as cues in item 8. Option *c* is correct because it states that burns *may* occur; however, it is not a necessary outcome.

9. This question allows you to eliminate option *a* because of the poor grammatical match. By comparing each of the remaining options to the stem, we can figure out that the correct answer is *d*. Option *c* does not fit very well with the stem, and option *b* is incomplete.

10. Did you guess on this question? The correct answer is *a*.

Essay Tests

Essay tests are often considered the most difficult of all types of tests for two reasons; an answer must be *constructed* rather than recognized, and the way the answer will be graded is not clear. As a result, essay tests create challenges not present in other kinds of tests. Yet, essay tests need not be feared by an aggressive test taker. Essay tests offer an opportunity to maximize the use of the knowledge you have. For example, with essay tests you are in control of revealing what you know, and you may use what you have learned from many courses to improve your score on an essay question. Success on essay tests depends on developing and using your understanding of the course content, organizing that content well, and writing a clear, well-developed response that relies on your understanding and organization. The action principles in this chapter will help you write a good essay answer.

CHARACTERISTICS OF ESSAY TESTS

Essay questions are relatively easy to make up. This is one reason teachers like them. A more important reason many teachers choose to give essay tests is to see how well you can use your knowledge to develop and support a conclusion. Consider the examples below:

Question: The Compromise of 1850 averted a major crisis in American History. Describe the major elements of the Compromise of 1850 and the crisis resolved by the Compromise.

Answer: The Compromise of 1850 was presented by Henry Clay in February of 1850. It contained six essential proposals: (1) that California be admitted as a free state, (2) that the slavery issue in other territory acquired from Mexico be decided by popular sovereignty, (3) that the District of Columbia no longer be used as a depot in interstate slave trade, (4) that slavery be abolished in the District of Columbia only with the consent of the citizens of the District and Maryland, (5) that a new fugitive slave law be enacted, and (6) that Congress no longer interfere with interstate slave trading. This compromise, which was passed by Congress and signed by President Fillmore, averted secession by a group of southern states.

This example represents Type I learning (comprehension). It is mainly a list of elements of the Compromise of 1850.

Here is a second example:

Question: In the poem *Jabberwocky*, Lewis Carroll uses strange and unusual words. What do you think Carroll was trying to achieve by using these words in this poem?

Answer: Carroll was probably trying to create interest in the basic story of this poem by using unusual words. The story is a quest in which a boy seeks and slays a Jabberwock—essentially a type of story often told. Interest is generated in such a story by the author setting a scene, providing detail and drama. Carroll did this in an unconventional way by using nonsense words, such as *vorpal, fruminous, tulgey*, and *manxome*. The reader is free to attach any meaning to these words, to, in essence, use these words to make the detail of the story whatever the reader chooses.

This answer represents Type II learning (analysis). The question asks for an opinion that must be supported by referring to the poem.

ESSAY TESTS AND THINKING

Most professors are probably looking for a demonstration of something more than just repetition of facts on an essay test. But this is true for most tests, so we cannot say essay tests require more thinking than other kinds of tests. What then is different about essay tests?

Essay tests make three demands: You must construct a response; you must organize your answer well; and you must write the response. No other form of test places these three demands on you. With an essay test, you also have several advantages. You have complete control over what information in your memory you use or do not use, and you are in control of how you demonstrate what you know. To do well on an essay test, you do not need to know more than for other kinds of tests; you do need to demonstrate what you do know in a different way. It is the requirement of writing an answer that bothers so many students about essay tests. However, because you can control what you write, essay tests can be advantageous to you.

The following principles will help you respond to the three demands placed on you by essay tests.

Principle 4.1: Answer the question directly.

Your first task in answering an essay question is to answer the question as asked. Clearly state an answer to the question using the information you have studied. Notice in the *Jabberwocky* example that a direct and clear answer was given in the first sentence ("Carroll was probably trying to create interest in the basic story . . ."). The question was not repeated; no lengthy introduction of redundant material was used; a clear and straightforward answer was given. Your first goal with an essay question is to formulate a direct and concise answer. Once you have an answer, then develop support for the answer as was done in the *Jabberwocky* example.

In order to develop support for your answer, you must organize what you know into an effective statement and then write that statement.

Principle 4.2: Organize your essay answer.

No amount of information will help you get a good grade if it is not presented in an organized manner. Good organization is a key element in successful essay test taking. Developing good organization takes some thought and planning. Fortunately, you can usually predict most of the content of an essay exam and plan and develop an organizational framework before actually taking the exam. By nature, essay exams are very general and focus on general, rather than specific, issues. Therefore, you can assume that the major issues covered in a course will serve as the focus for essay questions. It is also a good idea to think of examples to illustrate each concept or topic. These examples should be drawn from the course lectures and reading material.

There are many ways you can organize to write an essay response, and there is no single best way. You must organize your response so that you can use the knowledge you have to your best advantage. Here are two examples of how an essay could be organized:

Organizing by time. When organizing by time, you trace the flow of events according to the time they occurred. This is a good way to develop a theme of the interconnection between events. For example, in a history course on the United States, you might be asked to describe the emergence of the

United States as a nation or the rise of nationalism. Your essay could be organized around the following dates:

1775	—Battle of Lexington and Concord
1776	—Declaration of Independence
1781–83	—Negotiations for Peace
1787	—Northwest Territories Organized
1789	—Washington's Inauguration
1791	—Bill of Rights
1792	—Washington Re-elected
1795	—Pinckney Treaty
1798	—XYZ Affair
1803	—Louisiana Purchase
1812	—War of 1812
1819	—Adams-Otis Treaty
1820	—Missouri Compromise
1823	—Monroe Doctrine

You could write your essay to describe the importance of these events and how they contributed to nationalism. Organization by time can be applied to essay questions in history, literature (to show the development of a form of writing, such as the novel), science (to trace the development of a theory over time) and any other subject.

Organizing by function. An essay may be organized by function. This is the way the chapters in this book are organized. We chose this organization because we felt it was the best way to help you prepare yourself to be an aggressive test taker. But we could have chosen another way to organize this information. You must choose a way to organize your responses that you think will best demonstrate what you know.

Essay exams require more than knowledge of the subject matter. Good writing skills are also necessary. You may be judged on your writing ability as much as on your knowledge. As a consequence, you must carefully construct your response so that you: (1) state a position on the question; (2) analyze the key elements of the issue and provide examples in your analysis that support your position; and (3) draw a clear conclusion(s) that is well supported in your analysis. Make your response very clear so there is no chance that the professor will misunderstand where you stand. Usually, it is not wise to waffle either. If you organize an accurate statement of your position and defend it, you will usually be quite successful with essay exams.

ESSAY TESTS AND GRADING

Many professors prefer essay exams because they are relatively easy to make up. An essay test requires relatively few questions to make a complete exam in comparison to a multiple-choice exam, which would require 50 to 100 questions. But, although easy to construct, essay exams are usually quite difficult to grade. Student answers can vary widely, particularly when there is no single correct answer, as is the case with most essay questions.

Most professors grade essay exams according to criteria they select in advance. These criteria may be focused on any of the three types of learning we have discussed. That is, the criteria could call for the verbatim use of facts or a restatement of factual information, the manipulation of information, or problem solving. Since the criteria vary for different types of learning, the way you answer an essay question should be guided by the stated or implied criteria of your professor.

Principle 4.3: Discover the criteria that will be used to judge your answer.

Some criteria that may be used to grade an answer include originality, accuracy, imaginativeness, completeness, organization, writing skills, grammar, spelling, sentence structure, use of ideas, ability to identify critical issues, and use of detail. Because each professor has a unique set of criteria, you must find out what criteria *your* professor will use to grade your answers.

There are two basic ways to discover these criteria. The first is to ask the professor how the essay will be graded. Frequently, a simple question, ''What do you look for in an essay answer?'' will yield this information. Note the answer carefully and use the information to guide your study and your organization when writing. It is better not to wait until just before the exam to ask for criteria. Find out early in the course what criteria will be used.

The second method is less direct and more risky because it involves some detective work. If the professor will not reveal criteria, observe carefully what is stressed in class. If facts are stressed, you can assume that many facts will be looked for in your response. If analyses of issues are stressed, then this may be the focus of grading. You may also attempt to obtain previous exams from former students in the course. This has the advantage of letting you see some actual questions the professor asked and how they were graded.

As you prepare for a test, review the major ideas emphasized by the professor. Then organize these issues so that you can understand them.

Here is an example from physics:

Suppose in your class in introductory physics, your teacher has stressed the role of science as a means of studying physical phenomena. This probably included such elements as the purpose of theory, the development of theory, the scientific method, and the means by which questions may be investigated. Since the teacher has spent so much time on these ideas, you can assume they are important. It would be wise to prepare to respond to possible questions about the role of science. For example, one possible question could be: "Why do physicists develop theories about physical phenomena before they have all the facts? In your response, describe how physicists develop theories."

What criteria might be used to grade an answer to this physics question? Rarely do professors write out a full answer to an essay question. Ordinarily, they make a criteria list and then look for these elements in the response. You should follow the same procedure in developing your answer. For the above question, the following ideas would reasonably be included in your answer:

1. All the facts are never known, therefore it would be pointless to wait.
2. Theories help to identify facts that are unknown.
3. Theories are developed by
   a. Summarizing known facts,
   b. Predicting facts that are unknown,
   c. Organizing the above into a reasonable explanation.

Predicting criteria can have two benefits. First, it can provide you with a set of ideas to focus your study and actually use to write an essay answer. Second, you may be able to check the accuracy of your criteria with the instructor or fellow students.

Principle 4.4: Find out what the professor wants to see as evidence that you have learned.

This principle is essentially a restatement of the preceding two principles. We restate it to emphasize that a good part of being successful on an essay exam is demonstrating that you have met the purposes the professor has in mind. Essay tests are subjective because your grade depends upon meeting the professor's subjective criteria. If you know what the professor's goal(s) is, you will have a much greater chance of being successful. If the purposes are unclear, do not be reluctant to ask. Such questions as "Is your goal to help us understand how complex the development of a democracy is?" for example, will provide you with some understanding of the professor's purpose. It is a good idea to ask questions about whatever you perceive to be the purpose of the course, rather than to just ask "What is the purpose of this course?" However, if you cannot identify any relatively obvious purpose, then ask for a purpose statement (i.e., "What do you want us to get out of the course?"). As you attempt to determine what the professor wants for evidence, direct your search for criteria to major purposes of the course.

Here is an example from English literature:

> Rarely do English professors want you to state facts; they usually want you to interpret literature accurately. Thus, you might ask, "Do you want us to show we understand the use of symbolism in literature?" "Can we do this by identifying examples from one story, or should we be able to give examples from several things we have read?"

This is an example from composition:

> Usually, the purpose of composition classes is not that you remember grammar rules, but rather that you use grammar to communicate effectively. So, you might ask, "Should we memorize grammar rules or practice using grammar and sentence structure to express an idea?" "Is it more important to be grammatically correct or to be able to say why a sentence is correct or incorrect?"

These questions are about major course purposes and how you can demonstrate you have met these purposes. As an aggressive test taker, you must look for the important things, and you must also find out how you can show that you do know these things.

TAKING AN ESSAY TEST

In this section, we will cover some guidelines to follow when actually answering essay questions. We will begin by presenting the more important principles for aggressively attacking essay tests. In general, we suggest being sure you understand the test questions and that you organize and write thoughtfully. Use the examples to help you understand the principles, and try to remember some tests you have taken on which you would have been able to use the principles.

Understanding Test Questions

Principle 4.5: Read each question carefully.

Many essay questions will require you to discuss a relationship between two or more major issues. Make sure you know what issues are included in the question. Do not answer a question that was not asked. For example, look at this question:

> It has been stated that theory is a teacher's most useful tool. Defend or reject this statement.

The question clearly requires you to take a position and support it. You are not asked to catalog the reasons one might present to defend and reject the statement. Answering this question by giving reasons to accept and to reject the statement would be answering a question that was not asked. And, regardless of how well you presented these reasons, you probably would not do as well as you would have had you taken a position and defended it. So, if you agree with the statement, you should begin your essay in this way:

> Theory is a teacher's most useful tool. There are three main ways a theory assists a teacher to be effective: (1) theory helps a teacher understand students; (2) theory helps a teacher interpret new information; and (3) theory helps a teacher predict the consequences of his/her actions.

The rest of the essay could be organized into a discussion of the importance of each of these three functions of a theory.

Here is another example from history:

> Although a shooting touched off World War I, what were the real causes of the war?

This question appears to seek an analysis of the economic and political reasons that caused World War I. There is no need to describe the events surrounding the assassination of Archduke Francis Ferdinand, heir to the Austrian throne. Nor would it be wise to describe the problems of the Balkan states. Rather, the response should focus on the effects of industrialization, the competition for markets, and the growth of nationalism. This question illustrates an essay item that must be interpreted to determine the intent of the question. Since the word *real* appears in the question, it is quite likely the material was covered in class or in the text in terms of "real" causes of the war. These causes should be the focus of your answer.

Here is another example drawn from business law:

> Mr. Franks accepted a position as an auditor with the Acme Slumber Company, a firm that makes matresses. When hired, Franks signed an agreement that he would not accept employment with any of Acme's competitors for five years after leaving them. After only one year, Franks left Acme and accepted a position with another company whose products were very similar and whose markets were the same as Acme's. The Acme Slumber Company sued Franks for breech of contract. What would be the outcome of this case? Explain.

Here you are asked to do two things: predict the outcome of the suit and explain your prediction. You should begin your answer by stating what the outcome would be and then describe legal precedents to support your answer.

Principle 4.6: Seek clues to the answer from the question.

As you carefully read questions, also seek clues to the answer from the question. For example, consider the following question:

> A reason frequently given for asking students essay questions is that this form of test requires students to demonstrate how well they can think. The basis for this rationale is that students must construct, rather than simply recognize, a response. Do you believe that essay tests require more thinking than so-called objective tests?

This question actually lays out all the important issues for you by identifying the major pros and cons of two forms of tests. Your answer should discuss (1) the relationship between constructing a response and thinking and (2) the thinking required in recognizing a response. Notice also in the example from business law the statement, ''After only one year. . . .'' The word *only* here may be a clue to some legal precedents in contract law. Clearly, the word *only* is an indication that the contract was not fulfilled. Essay questions will frequently contain clues like these that may help you construct your answer.

Principle 4.7: Use work sheets to remember details.

Finally, as you read each question carefully, jot down ideas about each question as you read. We recommend that you develop a *work sheet* by writing the question number at the top of a blank piece of paper. Anytime you get an idea related to a question, write it on the work sheet. Use the work sheet to record immediately any formulas or critical information you have memorized. Do this right away before other ideas interfere with these memorized facts. Also, do not trust your memory to recall important ideas; write these down when you get them, even if you are working on another question. There is nothing more frustrating and defeating when writing an essay answer than losing an idea.

Principle 4.8: Define the question in a way you can write about it.

Some essay questions may be vague and poorly defined, requiring you to use your knowledge of the course to define the issues involved. If a question is vague, your first task is to define the question so you can answer it. For example, consider the following question from sociology:

Describe the impact of the concept of social welfare.

There are literally hundreds of ways to respond to such a question; the question is so vague and broad that one might despair of ever answering it adequately. When you find a question such as this on an essay exam, before doing anything else, you must define or restate the question in a reasonable and answerable form. Here, you must draw upon your knowledge from the course as well as your understanding of the professor's goals. Using this information, organize a statement of critical issues, and discuss these issues. For example, you could define *social welfare* and trace its impact on social services. Or, you could illustrate changes in legal, legislative, and judicial processes that have arisen as a result of social welfare. Or, you could describe society before and after the introduction of the concept of social welfare in terms of family relations, religious concerns, and social activism.

An example from history follows:

Discuss the effects of the Thirty Year's War on Europe.

This is another question that could be the subject of a long book. The question requires careful definition in order to be answered well. You might choose to discuss social effects on common people, commerce and trading effects, political effects, and religious effects, to name but a few.

How should the decision be made to answer in one way or another on essay questions that obviously need definition? The best essay test answer is one that relies on what was emphasized in class and demonstrates your own knowledge. Clearly, you want to define the question in a way that you can answer it. For example, if your sociology instructor emphasized family relations when discussing social welfare, then defining your answer in terms of family relations would be a good bet. The same is true for the history question; if the instructor emphasized political effects, then it would be wise to answer in terms of political effects. Of course, it is a good idea to acknowledge that there are many possible effects of the Thirty Year's War that could be discussed. Thus, you might begin your answer in the following way:

Clearly the effects of the Thirty Year's War on Europe were far-reaching. Any major conflict affects commerce, religion, politics, and day-to-day life. However, perhaps the most significant effects—those that most affected all of Europe and the rest of the world—were the political effects.

At this point, you could describe the main political effects in an organized way. By beginning your essay in this manner, you demonstrate that you have more knowledge than you are writing down and that you have carefully defined your response in a thoughtful and purposeful way.

There usually is no single right way to define a question. In fact, most essay questions are written so that they may be defined in a number of different ways. Remember to define the question *in the way that you can best answer it.*

Principle 4.9: Budget your time.

The first thing you should do is read and consider *all* the questions on the exam before responding to any single question. This allows you to budget time to each question in accordance with your knowledge and the time needed to answer each question. Usually, you should answer every question and not spend all your time doing a superior job on only one or two of them. This requires time budgeting.

Budgeting your time does not necessarily mean giving an equal amount of time to each question. Other factors should be considered. You will find that some questions are easier than others or can be answered more quickly. These questions should be given less time so you can devote more time to more difficult questions. It may also be that some questions earn more points than others. If this is the case, allow more time for the questions that count more.

Once you have made a decision on how much time to give each question, write down the time to be given to each question beside the question. Keep track of when you begin each answer, and follow your schedule. If you run out of time, go on to the next question. It is a good idea to budget five or ten minutes extra time to return to questions you had to leave unfinished. Of course, if you finish another question early, this will give you the time to return to an unfinished answer. The idea here is to use the time available to your best advantage; taking a few minutes to budget your time usually pays off.

Principle 4.10: Carefully order how you will respond to the questions.

It is a good idea to begin by answering the questions you know best. So, in addition to budgeting your time, decide the order in which you will answer the questions. You can note this order by writing a number beside each question.

You may choose to do a very difficult question first because you know the answer to that question. Whether the first question you answer is easy or hard, you must decide which is best for you.

Beginning with an easy question gives you an opportunity to quickly respond to one question and get it out of the way. This will usually build confidence and get you mentally prepared to tackle tougher questions. This method also gives you some time to relax and get over pretest jitters. The disadvantage of beginning with an easy question is that you still have the hard ones to attack and may use time to answer the easy question that you will need for the harder ones.

The advantage of answering a difficult question first is that you can get the worst out of the way. You can immediately use those hard-to-remember facts, and the rest of the exam will be much easier. Some people want to get the worst out of the way first.

Whatever you choose to do, remember that you can control the order in which you respond to essay questions. You should judge the difficulty of every essay question in order to budget your time and decide the order in which to answer questions. Regardless of whether you start with an easy or hard question, *always* begin with a question that you know how to answer.

WRITING YOUR RESPONSE

Principle 4.11: Use the technical language of the subject.

Use technical terms or the language regularly used by the professor and the text and be accurate in the use of this language. For example, do not use a phrase like "We give tests to see what students learned," when you could say "The purpose of tests is to evaluate student learning." Use of technical language and content-related terms is usually considered an indication that you have mastered the content.

Here is another example from English literature. Suppose you were given this question on the play *The Miracle Worker*, by William Gibson.

Describe how the abstract and concrete work together in *The Miracle Worker*.

You might begin your response as follows:

At the beginning of the play, Kate discovers that her baby is deaf and blind from illness.

Although the sense of the above statement may be correct, it may be better to begin your answer using technical language as follows:

> In the prologue of the play, Kate discovers that illness has left her baby blind and deaf.

In the second example, the term *prologue* is used. Use of this technical drama term tends to indicate a higher level of knowledge than would be shown if the term had not been used.

One more example of the use of technical terms is drawn from organizational management. Consider the problem below:

> Explain what happens to organizations as they grow and gain experience and strive to meet established goals.

One answer to this question could begin in this way:

> As organizations grow, different elements of the organization begin to perform more specific functions. The elements then become subunits with separate organizational structures of their own.

As in the previous example, this answer may be essentially correct. However, it does not use the technical terminology often used in the study of organizational management. Here is a better beginning to the response:

> As organizations grow and gain experience, they tend to *progressively differentiate*. This *progressive differentiation* is reflected in subunits becoming more specialized in their functions and individuals being responsible for fewer tasks.

The use of the term *progressive differentiation* indicates a deeper level of knowledge and familiarity with the subject matter.

These examples represent only the first sentence or two of what would be a much longer response. Technical terms should be used throughout your response when appropriate.

We are not advising you to play with words in an attempt to be impressive. If you understand the language of a subject accurately, it is a clear indication that you do understand the subject. As an aggressive test taker, you should be alert to the meanings of technical terms and use these terms in your answer. Many times it is just not possible to express yourself well without using these technical terms in a precise way.

Principle 4.12: Use facts to support your arguments.

Nothing is more impressive than to state a well-organized opinion and then to support that opinion with appropriate facts. While it may not be necessary to overkill with lots of facts, you should use facts as examples to support your position. Sometimes it is good actually to quote an authority verbatim. Learn important quotations that have the potential for being very useful. Such quotes are usually drawn from a key source and are widely applicable in many contexts. For example, the "All the world's a stage" passage from Shakespeare could be used to support many arguments about Shakespeare. As professors ourselves, we are occasionally impressed when a direct quote is woven into an essay to support a major point.

In essay answers, include several kinds of facts. In the social sciences, for example, you might commit to memory a particularly important study. The same is true for physics, chemistry, or any of the physical or social sciences. In literature, you could remember an example that illustrates a revolutionary or new way to use language or form of expression. In art, you could seek out examples of new ways that a particularly influential artist used to express an idea or emotion. We are suggesting, here, that you identify very important events associated with the subject you are studying. Learn these facts well—well enough to quote word-for-word in some cases. Then as you write your answer, use the facts to support ideas you are presenting. Following are some examples.

An example from physics:

> Before the first decade of the 15th century, physicists generally believed in a particle theory of light. A French engineer named Augustin Fresnel proposed a wave model, which was in direct contradiction to the common beliefs of scientists. Fresnel's model was rigorously challenged by a man named Poisson, who predicted that if a certain experiment were conducted Fresnel's model would be disproven. Fresnel took up the challenge and produced results that contradicted the particle theory. As a result, the particle theory was abandoned in favor of the wave model. This important experiment changed the thinking of physicists on the nature of light. It is an example of an important experiment because it resulted in major changes in how physicists thought about light.

An example from art:

> Pablo Picasso used his artistic talent to express outrage at an incident during the Spanish Civil War and his horror of all war. His poignant *Guernica* (1937) proved to have a major influence on art and artists,

both on the selection of subject matter appropriate for art and on the manner in which emotion may be expressed. Knowledge of this work of art may serve as a useful reference point to discuss many movements and trends in art during the latter portion of the 20th century.

Guernica represents an important event in the world of art and as such may serve as a useful "fact" to aggressively support an opinion or idea in an essay answer.

WRITING AN ESSAY ANSWER

Let us briefly review the principles for writing essay answers. We have discussed twelve principles, eight of these related to writing an essay answer:

Principle 4.5: Read each question carefully.
Principle 4.6: Seek clues to the answer from the question.
Principle 4.7: Use work sheets to remember details.
Principle 4.8: Define the question in a way you can write about it.
Principle 4.9: Budget your time.
Principle 4.10: Carefully order how you will respond to the questions.
Principle 4.11: Use the technical language of the subject.
Principle 4.12: Use facts to support your arguments.

In addition to these principles, in Section 1 of this chapter and in Chapter 2, we have emphasized the importance of being well organized.

In the example below, we present a detailed account of how an essay exam can be attacked aggressively and how an answer could be written. We will present in parentheses the thoughts of an aggressive test taker as the test is attacked.

This example is from English literature. The test covers content on a unit of the course on the short story.

Here is the test:

Test Directions: Respond to each of the three questions below. You may use no reference sources and must turn in your paper promptly at the end of the class period (11:15 A.M.) Each question counts 1/3 of the total test grade.

1. We have analyzed short stories in class in an attempt to identify the major elements of a short story. What are these elements, and how do they contribute to a short story?

2. "The Lady or the Tiger?" was presented as an excellent example of the workings of a plot. Describe the major plot elements of this story, and describe how these contribute to the plot.

3. The story "The Ambitious Guest" employs the theme of personal ambition and the ironic twists of fate that determine the outcome of our dreams. Describe how Hawthorne uses symbolism to represent and develop this theme.

TABLE 4.1
Reading the Questions

Principle	Student Action
4.5 Read the questions	First, I will make three work sheets—now, to read the questions.
4.7 Write ideas on work sheet	We have analyzed short stories in class (make a note on work sheet that the answer should come from class activities) to identify major elements of a short story (yes, I know what they are, write down plot, setting, and character). What are these elements (wait, I believe conflict should also be included as an element, write it down) and how do they contribute to a short story?
4.9 Budget time 4.10 Evaluate difficulty	(This question is not too difficult and shouldn't take long to answer. I'll go on to read the second question.)
4.7 Write ideas on work sheet	"The Lady or the Tiger?" was presented as an excellent example of the workings of a plot. (This was done mostly in class, so the majority of this answer should also come from class. Hey, this question confirms part of my answer to question 1—*plot*: I'll use this story to get some examples—better write this on my work sheet.) Describe the major plot elements of this story and describe how these contribute to the plot. (I remember lots of conflict in this story, better write down *conflict*. Here I need to work out the major conflicts and relate them to sections of the story—write that down.)
4.9 Budget time	This will take some time, although it is not too difficult.
4.10 Evaluate difficulty	(Now, the last question—this is pretty easy so far.)
4.5 Write ideas on work sheet	The story "The Ambitious Guest" employs the theme of personal ambition and the ironic twists of fate that determine the outcome of man's dreams. (I remember this story was based on actual incident—better make a note, it may be important.) Describe how Hawthorne used symbolism to represent and develop this theme.
4.10 Evaluate difficulty	(Whew, I'm drawing a blank here; I'll have to reconstruct the story to find some symbols; if not, I'll have to write about the general topic of symbolism in short stories—write down these ideas.)
4.11 Time budgeting	I'll have to save number 3 to the last, I'll also need more time; I can do 1 in about ten minutes, easy; and 2 will take about ten minutes. That leaves twenty five minutes for 3; I'll leave five minutes in case I get tied up. Write times on work sheet.
4.10 Ordering responses	I'll start with 1, then 2, and last 3.
8 Definition	(First, I'll work out a clear definition of this question. This is really straightforward; it's asking for information with no opinion or interpretation. I'll just objectively write the answer.)

TABLE 4.2
Organizing an Answer

Principle	Student Action

4.2 Organize answer	(How shall I organize? It is obvious the best way will be around the three major elements—conflict is part of plot. What I'll do is discuss each element and subelements and then relate each to a purpose. Quickly outline on worksheet.)
	I. Intro
	   A. SS has three elements
	      1. Plot
	      2. Setting
	      3. Character
	   B. Three elements are held together by theme; that is, contribute to theme
	II. Plot
	   A. Series of related incidents
	   B. Includes conflict
	   C. Elements of plot
	      1. Exposition
	      2. Crisis
	      3. Climax
	III. Setting
	   A. The location of story
	   B. Provides symbolic information (What was story I read in high school that used jewelry as a symbol of wealth—"The Necklace." Write this down.)
	IV. Character
	   A. Motives
	   B. Traits
	V. Conclusion
	   A. Elements contribute to general framework of story.
	   B. Elements serve to reveal theme and moral of story.

4.5 Use work sheet	

TABLE 4.3
Writing an Answer—Example Response to Question 1

Principle	Student Action
4.1 Answer the question	A short story is ordinarily made up of three elements: plot, setting, and character. All three of these elements contribute to the theme of the story which expresses the author's main idea.
4.2 Reflects organization	Each element will be discussed separately; first, I will define each element and, second, I will describe how each element can contribute to a theme.
4.11 Use of facts for support	*Plot.* The several incidents that make up a story form the plot. Most stories include some form of conflict in a story to create interest in the reader. Usually, the conflict comes at the beginning of the story, and the purpose of the story is to describe how the conflict is resolved. The plot must contain the why and how a story comes about. That is, the plot must tie together the events of the story.

TABLE 4.3 (continued)

Principle	Student Action
4.11 Technical term *4.12 Use of examples*	The plot usually begins with an exposition (e.g., the king's discovery of the young man's indiscretion in ''The Lady or the Tiger?'') and follows with a series of incidents leading to a crisis or climax where the conflict is resolved.
	Setting. A story must take place somewhere and at sometime. This is the setting. The setting can contribute to the theme or the story in several ways.
4.11 Technical term *4.12 Use of examples*	The setting may function as a symbol, as in ''The Cask of Amontillado''; the setting may merely be an unimportant element or it may be almost a participant in the story, as in ''The Interlopers.'' *Character.* The characters are the actors in the story. The reader is always attempting to understand the motives and actions of the story's characters.
4.11 Technical term *4.12 Use of Examples*	The theme of the story is revealed through the actions, thoughts, and discussions of the characters. The theme, for example, may be revealed by a debate over motives between two characters or by the constant reference to a trait or action of a character.
4.2 Organization in Conclusion	These three elements—plot, character, and setting—are the major components of a short story. These elements allow the author to establish and develop a theme, which results in the resolution of some conflict.

Note that the student used all the principles. The questions were carefully read, ideas were immediately written on a work sheet, time was budgeted, and an order of responding was chosen based on the order of difficulty of the questions.

The student did not spend a lot of time with question 3, although it was recognized that the question was difficult. It was smart not to spend too much time on this question, but to spend the time on 1 and 2. However, the student did recognize that the question was difficult (an important observation) and planned time accordingly. Also, notice that the student made a few suggestions (and wrote them down) about how the answer to 3 could be written. Again, this was a smart move typical of an aggressive test taker. Always look for ways to help yourself. Give yourself suggestions and assistance whenever you can. Many students do poorly on essay exams because they do not use the information they know to answer an essay question. Another example of using all your information comes later in this example when the student recalls a story read in high school which was an example of use of symbols.

Now let us look at the example answer. We believe this to be a good response; it should be judged an *A* or *B* response in most freshmen-level English courses covering the short story. Why?

• It is well organized.

• It is well written. (A clear introductory statement is made that responds to the question, and there is a statement describing how the answer will be written.)

• The answer follows the organization described in the first paragraph of the answer.

• The conclusion summarizes the response.

• Many examples were used.

• Appropriate technical language was incorporated into the response.

Look at the organization of the answer; the student chose to organize around the three major elements of a short story. This was a reasonable decision and served as a good way to organize and develop the answer. Perhaps this organization was obvious for this answer, and alternatives did not need to be considered. However, we recommend that you always consider different ways to organize an answer.

There are many ways an answer might be organized. Why would you choose to organize one way rather than another? So that you can best show what you know. In addition, you should select an organization for your response that will fit with the time available. Sometimes you may be forced to use a second or third choice in order to meet the demands of time and detail required on a particular essay test.

Let us examine some alternative organization strategies and see some reasons for selecting one or the other.

Alternative 1—Focus on theme. The theme alternative might be selected to answer question 1 by someone who wants to write a more general response because of uncertainty about exactly what the elements are. Thus, the emphasis would be shifted toward the theme and the role of theme in a short story; the theme could then be analyzed into several major elements. By redefining in this way and reorganizing, this student would be able to write an answer which would not be possible with the model answer's organization.

Alternative 2—Single story. A student who has special interest in and knowledge of a single story may wish to demonstrate such knowledge. By stating that the major elements are to be exemplified in the chosen story, the student can effectively develop a very complete answer which satisfies the intent of the item and also shows very extensive knowledge of a story.

Alternative 3—Lists. Perhaps for a student who is not a particularly good writer or who may have trouble remembering examples, a list of questions would be a good way to respond. The list organization does answer the question and avoids the necessity of using examples. For example, "Plot answers the questions: What's the story about? Why did this happen? How did this happen?" etc.

We are suggesting that you consider several ways to organize an essay response. Often, the organization that you recognize first will be a good starting point but may not be the best you could choose. Always try to organize your response in a way that will allow you to use your knowledge to your best advantage. Alternate ways to organize are particularly important when you are having trouble coming up with an answer. Rather than read and reread the question, experiment with ways to organize your answer. This will help you define the question so you can answer it.

Whenever you write a response, be sure to reread it. You should correct all errors in spelling, grammar, and punctuation, even if you must scratch out some of your writing. (Incidentally, a bottle of correction fluid is very good to take with you to an essay exam.) If you think of examples as you reread, try to incorporate them into your responses (writing on every other line makes this easier).

REMEMBERING THE PRINCIPLES

The mnemonic device R.D. Bud will help you remember the principles for writing an essay. The *R* stands for *read* (Principle 4.5); the *D* stands for *define* (Principle 4.8); and *Bud* stands for *budget time* (Principle 4.9). Think of R.D. Bud as a robot that helps you by ordering with technical language and facts. *Ordering* stands for the way you respond to questions (Principle 4.10); *with technical language* is Principle 4.11; and *facts* stands for Principle 4.12. R.D. Bud, who orders with technical language and facts, will help you to be an aggressive and more successful test taker.

THREE SUGGESTIONS FOR SUCCESSFUL ESSAY ANSWERS

The following suggestions may or may not be helpful in improving your grade. There is some evidence that following them may at least marginally improve your grade.

Suggestion 1: Place your response toward the bottom of the stack when turning in your exam.

There is sometimes an advantage in not being the first exam to be graded because the first few exams are frequently graded more harshly. As the professor reads more and more exams, the tendency is to become more lenient.

This happens because the standard of comparison or grade criteria generally decreases to the level at which students are writing.

Suggestion 2: Write *more,* rather than less.

Because longer responses are generally judged more favorably than shorter responses, attempt to use all the time you have. A possible problem here is that you may write more than you know if you just pad the response. Doing this can be disastrous. Write as much as you can, but not more than you know. However, you should never sacrifice organizational time in order to write more. Good organization should always be your top priority.

Suggestion 3: Write neatly and on lined paper in ink.

Solid research indicates that those who write neatly get better grades than those who do not. The appearance of your paper—margin straightness, letter formation, writing on the line, lack of scratch outs, legibility—contributes to your grade. Writing as neatly as you can may make the difference between a *C +* and a *B*. Of course, most of the time illegible answers will be counted as incorrect.

PREPARING FOR AN ESSAY TEST

Essay tests require some different abilities than do objective tests. The following principles should help you prepare for essay tests by improving your ability to organize and write a good answer consistent with your professor's goals.

Principle 4.13: Practice answering questions on main issues.

Do not postpone consideration of main issues until you face your exam; try to think of some possible questions throughout the course, and practice answering them. There are several ways to make up possible essay questions. One way is to identify main issues raised in class. For example, if a history professor often relates events to economic issues, an essay question concerning the impact of economic factors on some event or events is likely. Thus, you could practice developing an economic analysis of key issues covered in the course. Another way to think of possible questions is to ask the professor or other students for copies of previous tests. You can practice developing well-organized answers to these questions. A third procedure is to discuss the course with fellow students and together try to predict what the questions will be about. An advantage of working in a group is that several people can develop answers that all of you may discuss. The focus of these discussions should be on the quality of the answer (use of facts, technical language, etc.) and the way the answer is organized. Although you may not be able to predict the actual questions on the exam, you will have gained much practice in organizing and applying the course content. This practice will clarify issues in your own mind and greatly increase your speed and success as you answer actual essay questions.

One very good practice is to develop position statements on main issues or concepts included in each course. These position statements could be the beginning sentences to essay questions you predict you might be given. The value of such statements is that you have prepared the focus of your response and need only develop and support your position.

Principle 4.14: Learn the professor's point of view.

A good part of being successful on an essay exam is knowing what is expected of you. Learn at the outset of the course what the professor expects, and orient your study to these expectations. For example, if the professor wants you to use many facts, then learn many facts to include in your essay. You can discover a professor's expectations by asking what will be looked for when the essay is graded. Or, you might ask students who have completed the course how essays were graded. Do not focus on whether the professor was a ''hard'' grader; try to find out the criteria used to grade the essay.

Principle 4.15: Seek item or question options.

If you have a chance, always request alternative questions. The reason is relatively obvious; the more questions available, the more likely you are to know the answer to one of the alternatives.

Principle 4.16: Develop organizers of the course material.

The importance of organizers has been repeatedly stressed. The development of organizers should begin as you study. An organizer is essentially an identification of main issues and other related issues. Organizers can be developed in several ways, but the most commonly known procedure is the *outline*.

The strategy with an outline is to identify main topics or headings and then include subtopics or headings under them. A completed outline describes the relationship between main topics as well as a summary of subtopics under each heading. Organizers like this appear in the beginning of chapters in many textbooks. If a book has behavioral objectives or pre- or postchapter summaries, these may also serve as organizers, which you may expand as you study.

Organizers are important for essay exams because an essay must be written in an organized way. But there is another reason for developing organization—psychologists believe that organized information is more completely remembered for longer periods of time. It is simply easier to remember related information than isolated facts. By developing organizers or outlines of the information you study, you will help prepare for an essay exam in two ways: (1) well-organized notes make it easy to practice responding to probable questions; (2) you will probably remember more of what you study longer.

SUGGESTIONS FOR DESPERATE SITUATIONS

The following two suggestions are for the desperate student who has not studied, organized, rehearsed, or questioned. We recommend them only to the desperate, but if you happen to get caught with a question you cannot answer, the suggestions could be worth considering.

Suggestion: Write something you know.

Do not ever display complete ignorance. If you should get caught with a question you truly know nothing about, redefine the question into one you can answer. Although you may indicate little knowledge about the topic of the question, you have at least demonstrated that you are not totally ignorant. If you are clever in the way you redefine the question, you may do quite well with this approach. The real problem is in discovering the essence of the question. Do not focus on specific issues as much as on the relation expressed in the question. For example, consider the following question:

Humor is often associated with pain in drama. Explain.

We could say this question is about drama and the sense of pain in humor. However, if we know little about drama, we might redefine the question as an analysis of paradoxical relationships or the presence of paradoxes in nature. In either case, an extended discussion could avoid the specifics of drama and focus on the general issue. It is hard to predict how such an approach will fare; yet, it is almost certain to be more successful than no response or one that displays total ignorance.

Suggestion: Write elliptically.

It is sometimes possible to use a single idea and continually restate it in many different ways. In an essay exam, this may be a way to generate a response when you do not know an answer. There are several ways to do this. One way is to repeatedly restate the question given by the instructor and comment on the question each time. Another is to just launch into a discussion of the merits of the question and thoroughly analyze the question. A third method is to relate current, popular, or unrelated events to the question and discuss these in your essay. You should be aware that there is nothing worse than to hand in a poorly written essay that is unrelated to the course. Following this suggestion may lead to disaster if you are not a pretty clever writer.

SUMMARY

Essay tests are often given by teachers because they are easier to prepare and require an answer be constructed rather than recognized. Prepare for an essay test by practicing well-organized thinking on the topic. Four principles that will assist this preparation follow:

Principle 4.1: Answer the question directly.
Principle 4.2: Organize your essay answer.
Principle 4.3: Discover the criteria that will be used to judge your answer.
Principle 4.4: Understand how you can demonstrate what you know.

In writing an essay response, carefully and aggressively seek to use what you know to construct an answer. Practice the following principles, and commit them to memory.

Principle 4.5: Read each question carefully.
Principle 4.6: Seek clues to the answer from the question.
Principle 4.7: Use work sheets to remember details.
Principle 4.8: Define the question in a way you can answer it.
Principle 4.9: Budget your time.
Principle 4.10: Order your responses.
Principle 4.11: Use the technical language of the subject.
Principle 4.12: Use facts to support your arguments.

These four principles will help you prepare actively and aggressively for an essay test by practicing and finding out what you will need to know in order to do well:

Principle 4.13: Practice responding to probable questions.
Principle 4.14: Learn the professor's point of view.
Principle 4.15: Seek item or question options.
Principle 4.16: Develop organizers of the course material.

Finally, if it should happen that the test samples knowledge you do not have or have not had sufficient time to develop, then the following suggestions may be helpful. (Only use them in desperation!)

Write something you know.
Write elliptically.

Essay tests offer aggressive test takers an almost unlimited opportunity to use all of the knowledge they have. By attacking questions in an organized and systematic manner, aggressive test takers will surely find essay tests to be a good opportunity to demonstrate what they know.

Action Practice

Essay tests require that you remember information, organize that information well, and write an answer that is to the point, clear, and logical. To help you apply the principles presented on essay tests, consider the essay question below.

Briefly summarize the conditions that resulted in the depression of the 1930s, and explain why these conditions resulted in severe economic problems.

How would you organize your answer? The question appears to have two parts: the reasons for the depression, and an explanation of why these conditions led to a depression. The answer, then, must have at least two parts.

Below are two answers to this question. Analyze each to determine whether or not the principles described in this chapter were employed. Pay particular attention to organization of the answer, use of information, and the quality of the writing.

Response 1
Severe economic problems came from declining agricultural prices. Overproduction in industry also contributed to the severe economic problems. Because of overproduction, workers were laid off, and unemployment increased (which was made worse by technological advances that replaced many workers with machines). The stock market also crashed because many investors tried to avoid losing money by selling stocks. The more stocks that were sold, the lower the stock prices fell. Soon there was no money left for investments.

Banks and businesses went out of business, which resulted in many people losing lots of money. The resulting mess was so bad that it took many years to rebuild the economy.

The answer does not begin with a good topic sentence that answers the question. Although the answer does summarize reasons for the depression, these reasons are not organized in any clear way. Can you think of a better way the answer might have begun? Perhaps a sentence such as this would have been better: "There were four main conditions that resulted in the depression of the 1930s." This sentence organizes the answer for the reader by telling what is coming later.

Response 1 is essentially a list of four conditions not tied together by any central theme. The answer basically represents Type I learning because there is no interpretation of conditions or organization of material.

Response 2

The Great Depression was partially the product of many economic problems, which created a cycle of overproduction, unemployment due to production cuts, and slumping sales due to unemployment. However, conditions such as these had occurred previously without causing a depression. It was the combination of these economic woes with the stock market crash in October, 1929 that plunged the United States into a deep depression.

Fluctuations in economic strengths were not uncommon in the economy of the United States; these normal fluctuations are what initiated the chain of events that led to economic collapse. In the 1920s, agricultural prosperity had declined due to postwar overproduction and low prices. At the same time, many businesses sold stock to expand production capabilities, creating a larger capacity for production than markets could support. Technological advances also were proceding rapidly, which resulted in unemployment. Because of these economic pressures, prices were rising while wages were falling and unemployment increasing.

On top of this already declining economy of the late 1920s, the failure of the stock market delivered a mortal blow to the economy. Since the economic decline was accompanied by a decline in stock prices, the thousands who had speculated through buying on margin began to sell their stocks in order to minimize their losses. This selling of stocks soon reached a panic stage in October, 1929, when more than 28 million shares of stock were dumped in less than a week. Stock prices plummeted; banks were unable to collect on loans; and many banks were forced to close. The result was a general loss of confidence in business and banking, resulting in further unemployment and deeper economic troubles.

The combination of a cyclical downturn in the economy and the crash of the stock market created severe economic problems that would take years to correct.

In this answer, a carefully developed theme of economic interdependence appears in the first paragraph. At the same time, the question is answered. The second paragraph provides support for the effects of this interdependency by summarizing the economic conditions. The third paragraph supports the answer to the second part of the question. The last paragraph restates the conclusion presented in the first paragraph.

Response 2 appears to be better because it is more clearly organized. It is also more complex than Response 1 and demonstrates Type II learning. The issues are not only stated, but are analyzed and combined into a position statement on the cause of the depression. Notice also that the second answer includes many more facts and uses more technical language than the first. In these two answers, we see the same basic information being used in two very different ways and, as a result, demonstrating very different types of learning.

Writing a good essay response requires that you include in the answer all the relevant information you possess. This includes facts as well as your knowledge about relationships between facts and reasons for outcomes.

To practice, analyze some essay responses you have written to determine if you used all the relevant information that supported your position. If not, look for ways to add to the answer and improve it. Further analyze your answers for use of the action principles, and look for ways to apply those principles you did not use into an improved answer.

Open-Book Tests

Open-book tests are significantly different from every other kind of test in that you are allowed to use some reference materials during an examination. You may be allowed to use any resource or only limited resources, such as only the course textbook or class notes. Open-book tests usually require essay responses, and preparation for open-book tests should be quite similar to preparation for essay tests with several important additions. The main addition is preparation of reference materials before taking the test. However, as with essay tests, good organization is essential, and familiarity with course content and purposes is mandatory.

CHARACTERISTICS OF OPEN-BOOK TESTS

Some professors prefer open-book tests because they are more like the way we use information in real life. When we must answer a question for ourselves or solve a problem outside of school, we are not ordinarily restricted from using any information that we believe will be useful. In open-book tests, your ability to obtain information from appropriate sources is tested as well as your ability to organize and use the information to write an answer.

Open-book tests may be taken either in class or out of class; the out-of-class type is usually called a take-home test. Take-home exams provide you with unlimited time. Therefore, a major reason for giving a take-home exam is to make possible the development of a solidly supported, well-organized substantive response to a difficult question or issue.

The open-book exam eliminates almost every objection to examinations posed by students. (1) Open-book exams do not require rote memorization and directly repeating text or lecture material. (2) When the test is taken home, the objection of insufficient time is eliminated. Although there are several advantages to open-book tests, there is one considerable disadvantage—they are almost always graded very rigorously. The reason is fairly obvious; since you are allowed to use reference sources, you are expected to provide a better organized and documented answer.

Open-book tests pose something of a dilemma for students. Although they eliminate many of the restrictions most of us object to when we take examinations, what would have been an excellent response under standard conditions may be judged only ordinary on an open-book test. Part of this dilemma can be resolved by separating open-book tests from take-home tests. The purposes of the two are different enough to justify this separation.

Take-Home Tests

Take-home exams are really very similar to an assignment to write a term paper or documented theme. The instructor is usually seeking a well-written and organized answer that takes advantage of the time and resources available under take-home conditions. In many ways, this type of exam provides you with an excellent opportunity to demonstrate what you know because you have both time and resources. Knowing that your answer will be graded rigorously, you can develop your answer with extra care. We know of only one way students can get into trouble with the take-home test—not studying for it. Take-home tests require just as much preparation as in-class tests, and the preparation must precede the test, just as with an in-class test.

In-Class Tests

The in-class, open-book test presents some additional problems for the student. In-class, open-book tests are usually graded more harshly than closed-book tests. Second, many students come to the open-book test poorly prepared. Third, much greater accuracy is usually demanded on in-class open-book tests. Actually, in-class, open-book tests require just as much preparation as closed-book tests and are generally more difficult, requiring very well-organized and documented responses. Because of the time constraints on an in-class, open-book test, you may only have time to use open-book resources to check or verify information used to support your answer. Thus, you have to attack the test just as you would if it were not open book. You simply will not have the time to develop an answer by searching through reference materials.

Principle 5.1: Prepare for an open-book test.

Open-book tests are not intended to be easy; they require as much preparation as any other test. Whether the test is in class or a take home, you will not have sufficient time to develop a well-organized answer without considerable preparation.

Principle 5.2: Find out why you are being given an open-book test.

The reasons for giving open-book tests vary. Your instructor may wish to see how well you can use a reference source, how accurately you can document your ideas, or how well you can summarize and organize information from the course into a good essay. Your instructor may also merely wish to save you the trouble of memorizing such information as formulas, facts, or details. Find out why you are being allowed to use reference materials so that you can prepare for the test in an appropriate way.

Open-book tests may not always be essay tests; you could be given an open-book multiple-choice test, matching test, etc. Whatever the form of the open-book test, prepare using the principles suggested in the chapters on the type of test you will be given.

TAKING AN OPEN-BOOK TEST

There are three principles you should use to avoid the problems many students encounter when taking open-book tests.

Principle 5.3: Do not over-answer the question.

There is a tendency with open-book tests to try to include too much in an essay answer by showing you have read *all* the relevant information. Answers to open-book examinations should be well organized, concise, and direct, just as with closed-book tests. Your goal is to be more accurate and more extensive with your use of supporting evidence for your arguments. You do not need give more lengthy answers by including moderately related or unrelated information.

Principle 5.4: Do not use extensive quotations.

On open-book tests you can frequently be trapped into using the words of an expert rather than your own. However, answers consisting largely of quotations only indicate that you can read and copy from a book. Most instructors are interested in how well you can write a well-illustrated answer supported by facts. You cannot do this if you use all your time and space to quote from your books. As with closed-book essay tests, construct your argument carefully and in your own words; use your resources to make sure your facts and examples are accurate. Use direct quotations sparingly.

Principle 5.5: Use your time well.

If the open-book test involves the recognition of correct answers, such as on a multiple-choice test, matching test or true-false test, answer *all* the questions you know with certainty first without using your book. On the remaining questions, rule out the obviously incorrect alternatives, and then check the remaining alternatives. You simply will not have enough time to check all alternatives for all questions. Therefore, you should begin by checking the alternative most likely to be correct; if it is correct, mark the answer and move on to the next question. If it is incorrect, check the next most probable alternative, and so on, until you have the correct answer. Also, save the most difficult questions until you have answered the easier questions.

PREPARING FOR OPEN-BOOK TESTS

Do not take an open-book test without prior study, whether it is a take-home or an in-class test. Poorly prepared students have to hurriedly flip back and forth through books and notes searching for an answer. Most often the search is futile because students who have not studied do not know what they are looking for or where to find it and probably would not recognize the answer even if they saw it. In addition, it is a very rare open-book test that will ask for answers that are found easily in either a book or class notes.

Principle 5.6: Prepare organizational summaries of the course content.

This principle represents the major positive and aggressive action you can take to prepare for open-book tests in addition to the action principles presented in the other chapters on the different kinds of tests. The idea is to develop a handy reference guide or index to help you find important material quickly as you write your answer. Of course, you should also use any already available reference guide, such as the book index, glossary, and table of contents. Create an indexing system of your knowledge that is keyed to the course—similar to the index in a textbook. The detail you will include in these summaries depends upon the purposes of your instructor for giving an open-book test. For example, if your teacher places great emphasis on facts and the use of supporting information, include references to many facts in your summary index.

The following are some examples of how you might develop these organizational summaries to assist you in locating information quickly.

Develop a topical outline and a cross-listing of text and note pages. For example, on a chemistry exam, one topic might be *effusion*. Your topic outline might look like this:

Topic	Notes	Text
Effusion	Feb. 11, 13	pp. 300–320
1. Definition	p. 25	p. 300
2. Purpose	p. 26	pp. 301–302
3. Equations	p. 26	p. 302
4. Experiments	pp. 27–28	pp. 305–10
a. Apparatus	p. 28	p. 305
b. Procedure	p. 28	p. 306–8
5. Importance	p. 29	p. 317–18
6. People (T. Graham)	p. —	p. 311–12

With this topic summary, you can quickly turn to the information in your book needed to illustrate an answer or to check an answer on effusion.

An issue or event index. Develop an index of important issues or critical events that have been discussed in the course, and cross-reference these to your notes and any other sources you may use during the test. For example, in history, the professor may have stressed the role of economics in world events. Your summary may look like:

Economic Effects	Notes	Text
1. Colonialism	p. 17	pp. 221–43
2. Colonialization		
a. Reasons for leaving	p. 20	pp. 301–10

Economic Effects	Notes	Text
b. Type of colony	p. 23	pp. 340–41
3. Nationalism	p. 40	
a. North Europe	p. 55	pp. 147–148
b. Southern Europe	p. 80	pp. 184–188
c. Others	p. 83	p. 238
4. Industrialization		p. 401
a. Europe		p. 321
b. America		p. 380
5. War	p. 30	
a. 16th Century	p. 32	p. 103
b. 17th Century	p. 43	p. 281
c. 18th Century	p. 71	p. 350

Develop an alphabetical index to supplement your book index. Study the index in your text or other books carefully. If the index is incomplete or fails to include issues stressed in your class, develop a supplement to the index, including the names, issues, facts, and so on that are not in the index, and include page numbers for them.

Prepare a formula index. When you will be required to use many formulas, prepare a list of these formulas, and index them to your notes and text in the same manner as a topic index.

Develop an index of summaries in a text or other sources. Almost every book includes summaries of the material in the book. These summaries can be very helpful to quickly review an idea or issue. Usually, these summaries are found at the beginning and/or end of chapters or major sections within chapters. Having these summaries marked or indexed may help you to develop your answer.

Develop brief written summaries of main issues or ideas. It may be helpful to take your practice answers to probable essay questions with you to the test. You might get a question you have already answered! If you prepare summaries of every major topic, you almost surely will be able to use some of the answers you have already written as summaries. You may also be able to combine one or two of these summaries into a single answer. If so, you will already have your answer organized; you will only have to write and illustrate your answer. We suggest that you note page numbers and events or facts that can be used to illustrate your answers at the bottom of these summaries.

The best way to develop a summary is the way that makes sense to you and will help you find the material you need quickly. Keep in mind that your goal for developing these summaries is for assistance in finding needed information quickly. We have seen a student put color-keyed tabs on the pages of a textbook. Each color represented a different topic; the tabs were put on pages that contained important information on the topic, and the information was written on the tab in an abbreviated form. This student did not waste a single minute looking for information.

SUMMARY

Open-book tests allow you to use reference materials. They may be given in class or may be taken home. The purpose of open-book tests is to determine how well you can use information sources to develop or construct an answer. These exams are usually quite demanding, and precision is ordinarily required for receiving a high grade. A take-home exam allows you the time and resources necessary to develop a substantive answer to a major question or issue. In-class, open-book tests usually eliminate the necessity to memorize important information (such as formulas or dates) not ordinarily committed to memory.

Since open-book tests are usually graded rigorously, special care should be taken to organize your response and to use information accurately. However, you should not over-answer by including information that is only partially related to your point or of only minor significance. The goal is to write a well-developed and well-documented response. It is more important that you use quality information than to only use information extensively. Lengthy quotations should be avoided so that you write an answer in your own words. As with any exam, you should budget your time in order to respond to each question as best you can.

Preparation for open-book tests should be as extensive and detailed as for closed-book tests. In fact, you should prepare more by developing organized summaries. These summaries will allow you to achieve the precision usually required. An advantage of open-book tests is that you can prepare probable answers in advance and take these to the test with you.

Action Practice

The major aggressive action suggested in this chapter was the development of organized information summaries. The usefulness of these summaries is not limited to open-book tests, however. These summaries may be used to organize and study for any test and to develop resources for writing assignments, such as research papers or analytic reviews. To develop your ability to prepare and use organized information summaries, try some of the following:

1. Choose a chapter from a textbook, and identify all the facts and

important pieces of information in the chapter. Develop an outline of the chapter including these facts and page numbers.

2. With a textbook in hand, but closed, think of several important facts that may be included in the textbook. Look these up as fast as you can using the table of contents and the index.

3. Follow the directions in exercise 2 to look up some important issues. You will probably find that issues are more difficult to locate. Develop an index to help you quickly find issue-related information.

4. Develop a summary of important events, discoveries, inventions, and so on that preceded a main event. Reference these preceding events to class notes and text pages.

5. Experiment with summarizing and organizing information. Find a method that is comfortable for you.

True-False, Matching, and Short-Answer Tests

True-false, matching, and short-answer questions are not as popular as essay and multiple-choice tests for several reasons. Questions for these tests are difficult to write and sometimes hard to grade. In addition, many professors do not believe that these tests provide evidence of learning equal in quality to that provided by essay or multiple-choice tests. However, because all three types of questions are frequently included as at least part of a test, you should become familiar with them. Each type of question has individual characteristics that require specialized test-taking strategies to get the best score.

TRUE-FALSE TESTS

Purposes of True-False Tests

Probably the most popular of these three test forms is the true-false test. True-false questions ask you to judge either the accuracy of a fact or the correctness of a relationship between two or more facts, events, or ideas. You must determine whether or not the fact is accurate or the correctness of the relationship between the two or more elements of the question. True-false test questions are usually presented not as questions, but as statements; your answer indicates whether the statement is true or false. True-false questions may be written to measure any of the three types of learning, although most true-false questions are either questions about facts (information) or relationships (manipulating information). The examples below illustrate true-false questions that measure different types of learning.

Thomas Wolfe wrote *Look Homeward, Angel.*

The formula for the mean is $\frac{\Sigma\ x}{n}$.

The protein coal of a virus is called copsid.

The placenta serves as an endocrine gland.

It is possible for an organism to have several brains.

Kipling was unhappy about his interview with Mark Twain.

These questions are straightforward statements of fact. Your task is to determine if the fact is true as stated. The following example includes both facts and relationships between facts.

The results of an increase in the proportion of males in the population are likely to be a higher crime rate, more unemployment, a higher percentage of crimes of violence, and more frequent wars. On the other hand, greater technological progress, more creativity and greater attention to social problems may also be expected.

Facts and a relationship between these facts are included in this question. All facts and relationships must be considered in order to identify the separate parts of the question. You must then determine whether or not the facts and the expressed relationship are true. In other words, you must determine whether an increase in the proportion of males would be likely to produce the results listed in the statement, given what you know about the role males assume in society.

Here is another example of a question that requires more than factual knowledge:

A perception of helplessness by a large percentage of the voting population is a viable explanation of why only 54 percent of the eligible population voted in the 1976 presidential election.

Here you must determine whether or not the perception of helplessness was present, whether or not it was strong, and whether or not this is a sufficient reason to explain why only 54 percent of the eligible population voted. True-false questions can be quite complex even though they measure information learning. The question below is an example:

The Medici family commissioned many great works of art when they ruled in England during the 19th century.

To decide whether or not this statement is true, you must ask yourself these questions: "Did the Medici family commission art works?" "Did they commission many?" "Did they rule England while commissioning the many art works?" and "Did this occur in the 19th century?"

Professors include true-false questions to give some variety to essay and multiple-choice questions and to test your familiarity with course material. When heavy emphasis is placed on facts in a course, you may get more true-false questions.

Principle 6.1: Discover what type of true-false question will be asked.

Preparing yourself to attack specific types of learning can be a tremendous advantage. It is important to know what kind of learning will be included on your tests. To discover what kind of true-false question will be asked, you may try several things. You may ask the professor what will be emphasized on the test. You may also request some sample questions. Obtaining copies of previous exam questions, if this is permissible, is yet another method. Finally, observe what is stressed during class sessions; if facts and factual accuracy are emphasized, then you can expect some factually oriented questions. If relationships are emphasized, focus your attention on how concepts are related to each other and the nature of the relationship.

To help you identify different kinds of questions, some additional examples of true-false questions are given below:

Type I Learning Examples

Examples from Biology
Some forms of diabetes are sex-linked.
A pyrimidine base contains a four-nitrogen ring.
There is a moderate correlation between sequency of chromosome puffs and gene action.

Examples from Art Appreciation
The main trait of Mannerist art is a shift toward the unnatural.
David's *Death of Socrates* has overtones to *The Last Supper*.
Cézanne was the founder of the pointillist style.

Type II Learning Examples

Examples from Biology
Experimental evidence tends to indicate that the breaking of dormancy in potato tubers is accomplished by depression of genetic material.
Neurospora is an ascomyceti characterized by a long diploid stage in its life cycle.

Examples from Art Appreciation
Baroque sculpture, like Bernini's, is different from Renaissance sculpture in that it makes the space around it seem inactive and dull.

Michelangelo's unhappy domestic life can be seen in the *Last Judgment* in which St. Bartholomew holds the shin of Michelangelo's mother-in-law.

Taking True-False Tests

True-false questions are not easily written because it is difficult to generate statements that are always true or always false. To be false a statement must *always* be false; to be true it must *always* be true. As a result, true-false items frequently contain either absolute or relative qualifiers. Such absolute qualifiers as *always* and *never* and such relative qualifiers as *usually* and *most of the time* can serve as cues in determining the correct answer to a true-false item.

Because a true statement must always be true, it is often necessary for professors to qualify items with relative qualifiers such as *usually*. Only by adding these qualifiers can the item be considered always true.

In some cases, statements may be given that are true sometimes and false sometimes. For example, consider this question:

The application of fertilizer promotes plant growth.

This item is true only under conditions of adequate moisture and proper soil conditions. However, because you may respond only by indicating whether the statement is true or false, you must respond to the question as written. The above example would be false because it is sometimes false. As you can see, aggressively responding to true-false questions requires some analysis of the question before making a judgment about whether it is true or false.

Principle 6.2: Look for absolute qualifiers; if one is present, the question will probably be false.

If a question contains *always* or *never* or another absolute qualifier, it is probably false. Almost nothing on earth can be accounted for in absolute terms. This is particularly true in the humanities, art, and the social sciences (history, sociology, psychology, etc.). In the physical sciences, however, some questions may include absolute qualifiers that are true, particularly when definitions are involved. For example:

Two hydrogen molecules and one oxygen molecule when combined always form water.

The answer here is true because, by definition, the compound of two hydrogen molecules and one oxygen molecule is water. You must use judgment in responding to questions with absolute qualifiers. However, when an absolute qualifier is included, it should be the focus of your judgment. Most questions with absolute qualifiers are more likely to be false than true. In making a judgment when you are unsure about a question with an absolute qualifier, try to remember if there is any reason for the item to be true. If you cannot think of any, then *false* is your best answer.

Since most professors are aware of the problems of using absolute qualifiers, you may not see many true-false questions that include *always* or *never*. We have included a few examples that include absolute qualifiers to help you become familiar with the way these qualifiers may be used in questions:

> Adenine is always linked to Thymine in nucleic acid. (This response is false even though it is from a physical science. It is an incorrect factual statement.)
>
> All hormones have an effect on what is termed a *target organ* or *organs*. (This statement is true and is related to a definition.)
>
> The chance of two independent events occurring together is always the product of the chances of each occurring alone. (This statement reflects a relationship and is true. Again, this relationship is true by definition.)

Principle 6.3: Look for relative qualifiers; a question with many relative qualifiers will probably be true.

When such qualifiers as *usually, most, normally, frequently,* and *almost never* are included in a statement, it may be either true or false. You must rely on your knowledge of the subject to determine whether or not the frequency of the issue merits the use of the qualifier. Because it is difficult to write statements that are always true, teachers use relative qualifiers. Therefore, when you see relative qualifiers in a question, focus your judgment on the accuracy of the qualifier. However, if there are several relative qualifiers in an item, it will probably be true. For example:

> Most politicians are honest.

This question may be either true or false depending upon the information used in judging both *most* and *honesty*. However, if the item were

> Most politicians are usually honest.

the only possible response is true because most people are honest more than they are dishonest.

Below are several examples in which relative qualifiers are used in true-false questions:

The *principal* form of citizen participation in this country, in regard to politics, is voting. (The term *principal* serves as a relative qualifier. You must decide: (1) Is voting a form of citizen participation? (2) Is it the principal form?)

Bureaucracies play a tremendous political role in our society. (Did you recognize the qualifier? *Tremendous* serves as a relative qualifier. Here *tremendous* serves as the focal point of the question, and you must decide if the role is, indeed, tremendous.)

The outstanding feature of Notre Dame is generally considered to be its twin towers. (The relative qualifier is *generally considered*, and you must decide whether or not the towers are generally considered to be the *outstanding* feature.)

The primary contributor to the Declaration of Independence was Thomas Jefferson. (The relative qualifier is *primary*; to answer true, you must believe Jefferson's contributions were greater than anyone else's.)

In *A Child's Christmas in Wales,* the chief winter activity of the boys was throwing snowballs at cats. (The relative qualifier is *chief.* You must decide whether or not the boys spent more time throwing snowballs than they spent in other winter activities.)

Principle 6.4: Longer questions are more likely to be true.

The length of a question can also serve as an important clue to its truth or falsity. Consider the question writer's problem for a moment. To write completely true statements, it is often necessary to include not only single-word qualifiers (*almost, sometimes, usually*), but qualifying phrases as well. On the other hand, false questions do not require qualifications. As a result, false questions often turn out to be noticeably shorter than true statements.

Principle 6.5: Answer the question asked; do not attempt to interpret it.

The natural tendency of all of us to interpret what we see and hear may cause special problems with true-false questions. Read each question carefully, and respond to it *as written*. For example:

Children from lower socioeconomic settings have lower achievement scores on standardized tests.

Many would respond true to this question because, generally, it is true that lower socioeconomic status is associated with lower achievement scores. However, the correct answer is false for an obvious reason. Some children from lower socioeconomic groups get high achievement scores. To answer true to this question, the test taker must interpret the question to read "Usually children from lower socioeconomic settings have lower achievement scores." This kind of question interpretation can only lead to problems.

You will be more able to answer each question as it is written if you carefully read the directions given for the test. Sometimes the directions will provide either some qualification or some direction in how to respond. For example, we found the following directions on a introductory physics test:

> Each of the statements below is either true or false. In the blank, write the word *true* if the statement is true according to our present thinking, knowledge, or accepted concepts. Write the word *false* if it is not.

Clearly, you should answer the items given in terms of "our present thinking, knowledge, or accepted concepts"—how the content was taught in the course. If the directions are unclear and qualifiers are confusing, ask your teacher if the statements are intended to be absolute.

Principle 6.6: If any part of a question is false, the whole question is false.

A question may be all true except for one fact or relationshp. If the question contains *any* false information, the whole question is false.

Below are some examples of true-false items with more than one part.

> The main concerns of all labor unions through history are better wages and better working conditions. (These two issues must both be "main concerns": better wages and better working conditions. If one was a main concern and the other was not, the item is false. Did you notice the relative qualifier *main*?)
>
> Following the Civil War, the 14th Amendment, or Due Process Amendment, was ratified. (In this question, there are three issues: Did ratification follow the Civil War? Is the 14th Amendment the same as the Due Process Amendment. Was the amendment ratified? If any of the three issues is false, the whole item is false.)
>
> Both plant and animal cells have large, water-filled vacuoles in their interior, but plant cells differ from those of animals by having a wall of cellulose on the exterior. (This item involves four decisions: Do both animal and plant cells have vacuoles? Are they in their interior? Do these cells differ? Do they differ by animals cells having cellulose on the exterior? The answers to all four questions must be positive for the answer to be true. If you know that both animal and plant cells do not have vacuoles, you could mark the response false without reading the rest of the question and save yourself some time.)
>
> In the third act of "Julius Caesar," the conspirators manage to gather around Caesar by petitioning him to free Metellus's banished brother. (In

this question there are two issues: Did this occur in the third act? Did the conspirators use the petition to gather around Caesar?)

Principle 6.7: If you do not know an answer, guess; you have a 50–50 chance of being correct.

There is rarely a penalty for guessing on true-false tests, so always guess even if you do not have time to read the question. Do not guess blindly, however, unless you must. Read the question, and guess the answer you think is most likely to be correct. You should always use what you know and other clues (such as question length) to make an informed guess.

Preparing for True-False Tests

Since true-false tests can and often do measure all types of learning, you should prepare as carefully for true-false tests as you would for any test. However, since many true-false questions rely heavily on factual information (Type I), pay particular attention to information learning. As you know, learning information well requires that you organize and summarize what you learn into major categories. Once you have established these categories, you can use them to file facts into your memory. Several short but concentrated preparation sessions during the two to three days preceeding the test should help you remember these facts for the test.

Your major goal in preparing to do well on true-false tests is to sharpen your skills in analyzing true-false questions into their facts and relationships. This sort of analysis is necessary to accurately determine whether or not all parts of a complex true-false question are true. We recommend that you practice this analysis of true-false questions.

MATCHING QUESTIONS

Purpose of Matching Questions

Matching questions involve associating or matching one term or concept with another. Ordinarily, matching questions will be presented in two columns, a question list and an answer list, with the direction that questions in one column be matched with answers in the other. Matching is an association task; the objective of these tests is to determine your familiarity with the concepts, personalities, key issues, facts, and so on that have been studied. Matching questions are not used frequently and are ordinarily only a portion of a larger test. Perhaps the most frequent use of matching questions is when an object, organ, or other pictorially represented object is to be matched with labels of its parts. An example is given in Figure 6.1.

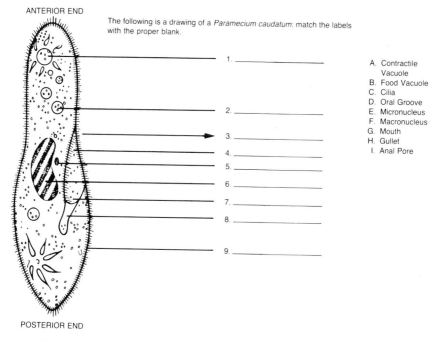

ANTERIOR END

The following is a drawing of a *Paramecium caudatum*; match the labels with the proper blank.

1. _____

2. _____

3. _____

4. _____

5. _____

6. _____

7. _____

8. _____

9. _____

A. Contractile
   Vacuole
B. Food Vacuole
C. Cilia
D. Oral Groove
E. Micronucleus
F. Macronucleus
G. Mouth
H. Gullet
I. Anal Pore

POSTERIOR END

FIGURE 6.1

Matching is a recognition test. You are given the question and the answer, and your task is to put the right answer with the right question. Ordinarily the matches will be straightforward and require little, if any, interpretation. But on some occasions matches may be quite complex, as when parts of an analogy must be matched with material you learned. Let us look at examples of both of these types of matching items to make this point clear.

The first example is from an introductory advertising course and requires the matching of definitions with terms; this question measures Type I learning. Your task is to determine which term belongs in which blank.

1. The speciality of copywriters and art directors. _____

2. The specialists who bring the advertisement from the design stage to the physical form required by the media. _____

3. Those who sell advertising time and space. _____

4. The specialist who participates in deciding what media should be used for a product, purchases the media, and evaluates the performance. _____

5. The specialists who measure the effectiveness of advertising and measure the size of the media audience. _____

6. The generalists who plan, implement, and control the advertising plan. _____

TERMS:

advertising researcher	media buyers
advertising producers	advertising creators
media sales representatives	advertising managers

The following example is drawn from an introductory psychology course and represents the matching of an analogy, requiring Type II learning.

Consider Freud's theory as similar to a horse-drawn cart with a horse, a cart, and a driver. Match the terms below:

1. horse   a. id
2. cart   b. ego
3. driver   c. superego

To successfully answer this matching question, you must understand Freud's theory and the role of the three elements in the theory. That is, you must answer this question, "Is the role of the concept of id similar to the role of the horse, the cart, or the driver?" It is fairly safe to assume that you will not see too many matching questions of this kind because they are extremely difficult to develop. In Figure 6.2 is another example of a matching question requiring Type III learning; this example is from an introductory biology test.

In the rainbow darter (a fish), sex determination is like that in man. Red (W) is dominant to white (w) and is sex linked. From the key list below, select the correct genotypes for the numbered individuals: square are males, circles are females. Match a number with each letter.

1. WW;   2. WY;   3. Ww;   4. wY;   5. ww

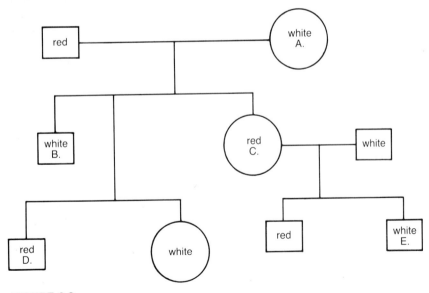

FIGURE 6.2

This question requires you to apply your understanding of the process of sex determination. In order to match the answer list (the numbered items) with the question list (the letters), you must understand the process of sex determination and the notation system (e.g., WW versus Ww).

Both of these last questions can only be studied for by using the best study skills and organizing your knowledge well. Most matching tests, however, will be focused on facts, and you should use appropriate study techniques to help you remember the facts you need to be successful.

Taking Matching Tests

Matching tests are not too difficult to answer since the task is deciding which member of the question list belongs with which member of the answer list. The following principles will help you in matching the members of the two lists.

Principle 6.8: Do the matches you know first.

Doing what you know first accomplishes two things. First, it gets these items out of the way, and second, it reduces the options for guessing on the items you do not know. You should begin by reading all of the question list *and* all of the answer list. Then answer the questions you know, first. Use your knowledge to do this, do not keep referring to the answer list. For example, consider the following matching question from an insurance class:

Match the following definitions with the correct term from the list below.

1. That condition that creates or increases the possibility of loss. _____

2. An economic institution that reduces risk by combining under one management a group of objects so situated that the aggregate accidental losses become predictable. _____

3. The contingency insured against; the event that may cause a loss. _____

4. The process by which an insurance company determines whether or not and on what basis it will accept our application for insurance. _____

5. The tendency of poorer risks of less desirable insureds to seek or continue insurance to a greater extent than do the better risks. _____

TERMS:

risk	risk avoidance	arbitration
peril	annuitant	adverse selection
hazard	randomness	all-risk
assumption	insurance	probability
contribution	underwriting	

As you read the question list and before reading the answer list, lightly pencil in the response you believe to be correct. Then as you read the answer list, cross out any terms inconsistent with the questions. This will reduce the answer list options to a small number (see Principle 6.10 below). Then return to the question list and answer each question, making sure the response you believe correct is one of the answer-list options. First answering the matching questions as you would if you were not given the answer list will save you time. Once you have answered all the questions you know, review those you do not know, and select the answer you believe to be best. Do your guessing last so you can benefit from having a smaller answer list.

Principle 6.9: Make sure you understand the directions for matching the items on the two lists.

In the example above from an insurance class, the answer list was longer than the question list. A good matching question always has more answers than questions; this prevents you from selecting a correct answer by the process of elimination.

Another important issue is whether or not an answer may be used *only once*. If so, cross it out as soon as you use it. When the directions do not clearly state whether or not you may use an answer more than once, quietly ask the instructor. This information is particularly important when you are struggling with a match for which an answer has already been used.

The matching question below is an example from introductory chemistry in which items from the answer list (included in the first sentence) may be used more than once. In fact, at least one answer *must* be used more than once in this example.

Indicate whether the following phenomena are examples of chemical, physical, or a combination of chemical and physical properties of the substance(s).

1. A metallic luster is observed when light shines on unoxidized iron. _____

2. Iron is placed in nitric acid (HNO_3) and hydrogen gas (H_2) release is observed. _____

3. Sulfur is heated to form a yellow liquid sulfur melt. _____

4. $CuSO_4$ (copper[ic] sulfate) dissolves in water to give a blue solution.
_____

5. Copper and tin are melted and mixed together to form the alloy bronze.
_____

Finally, make sure you understand how the matches should be made between the question list and the answer list. Usually this will be very obvious—matches may include authors with their work or labels with the appropriate object. But with a matching question involving analogies, however, the basis for making the match may be less clear. If you are unsure, quietly ask the instructor for an explanation.

Principle 6.10: Eliminate any items on the answer list that are incongruous or out of place.

Look for a common theme among the question list and the answer list. If all but two or three belong to one category, then the items that do not belong may probably be eliminated. For example, consider this question:

Match the author with his/her work.

E. Hemingway   *Lolita*
                The Old Man and the Sea
T. Robbins   *Another Roadside Attraction*
                All's Well that Ends Well
K. Vonnegut   *Slaughterhouse Five*
                Tom Jones
V. Nabokov

Here, *All's Well that Ends Well* and *Tom Jones* are very much out of place with the other items, which are novels written by contemporary authors. Attempt to determine what category the items included in matching questions belong to. Knowing the category will assist you in determining if all items belong, and, perhaps, reduce the number of options.

Principle 6.11: If you do not know the correct matches, then guess.

Like almost all tests, there is normally no penalty for guessing. Make as informed a guess as you can, but do not leave any items unmatched. Always guess after you have matched all the ones you know.

Principle 6.12: Answer long matching lists in a systematic way.

Most experts on making tests advise teachers to use relatively brief question and answer lists. Nine to twelve items in both lists is usually the maximum length for a single matching question. However, we have seen tests that included as many as fifty items on the question list and fifty items on the answer list. Frankly, an extremely long matching question is very difficult because of the limited ability of the human brain to remember so much information. To be successful on a long matching question, you must work systematically. The matching question below appeared on a test in an English course. Not all words have definitions listed.

Directions: Match the column on the right with the column on the left. Not all words have definitions listed.

_____ 1. hyperacidity	a.	excessive acid
_____ 2. hypothyroid	b.	high blood pressure, tension above the ordinary
_____ 3. hypertension	c.	deficient activity of the thyroid gland
_____ 4. homocentric	d.	every two hours
_____ 5. biochemistry	e.	to deny what has been said
_____ 6. anthropology	f.	not mingling with others
_____ 7. amoral	g.	length of a straight line through a circle
_____ 8. homocide	h.	belief in many gods
_____ 9. atypical	i.	top layer of skin
_____10. polygamy	j.	having similar centers
_____11. monotheism	k.	channel for conducting water
_____12. polysyllabic	l.	study of life's chemical functions
_____13. autobiography	m.	device for measuring short distances
_____14. homonym	n.	measures hearing ability
_____15. geopolitics	o.	study of men and their cultures
_____16. monarchy	p.	large device for projecting sound
_____17. monogamy	q.	study of a person's life written by that person
_____18. sociology	r.	science dealing with skin and its diseases
_____19. criminology	s.	false name
_____20. microfilm	t.	treats bone disease
_____21. intramural	u.	killing of one human by another
_____22. paternal	v.	consisting of different colors
_____23. dehydrate	w.	not like the ordinary (typical)
_____24. fraternal	x.	brotherly
_____25. omnipresent	y.	not moral
_____26. biennial	z.	marriages to several at one time

This extreme example will allow us to show how you may use at least one systematic strategy to respond to any long matching question. Of course, you must first remember and use the previous four principles. Begin at the top of the list, and attack each item on the question list in order. If you know what *hyperacidity* is with certainty, then look for the answer by beginning at the top of the answer list; continue sequentially through the list until you find the answer. Then cross it out or check it as having been used once; even if an answer may be used more than once, it is not likely a single answer will be used more than two or three times. Then go on to the next item on the question list. If you know for sure that you do not know what *hypothyroid* means, skip to the next item, *hypertension*. Once you have completed all the questions you know, begin working on the ones you *think* you know following the same procedures. Keep this up until you complete the whole question by guessing at the items you do not know at all.

PREPARING FOR MATCHING TESTS

If you know you will have some matching questions, you will probably be required to match facts. Since matching questions are usually only a small portion of a test, you will be devoting the majority of your preparation to preparing for the other types of questions to be asked (usually essay or multiple-choice questions). As you study, pay close attention to important facts, dates, events, people, and concepts that may be included in a matching question. Most matching questions do not include trivia, but focus on important topics and facts.

Use good study procedures, and organize your study in the ways discussed in earlier chapters. This will help you develop categories that will assist you in remembering specific facts. You may also wish to construct some association lists of facts, people, and so on from your course. A good practice activity is to scramble the lists and then match them. If you know you will have to match labels with parts of an organ or object, then you should frequently practice the task and check your answers. Do not think that because you got all the answers once you can do it again. Continue practicing until you can correctly label all parts three or four times on two or three separate days. If you are able to do this, you will probably have little trouble with matching questions. Of course, finding out what topics the matching questions will cover (e.g., dates and events, people and contributions, terms and definitions, authors and titles) will help you focus your study.

SHORT-ANSWER TESTS

Purpose of the Short-Answer Test

The purpose of short-answer questions is to test your recall of specific facts or other information. Short-answer items require you to generate or write an answer, like an essay test. This is in contrast to true-false, matching, and multiple-choice tests, which require you to recognize a correct answer from a list of alternative answers. Short-answer questions are usually included as a portion of a test that also contains other forms of questions, such as essay or multiple choice.

Short-answer tests are usually given to measure recall of facts, rather than interpretation of facts as in an essay test. Short-answer tests are relatively popular in courses stressing facts. They give the teacher a method to check how much you have read, studied, and paid attention in class. Therefore, questions on short-answer tests are usually focused on important facts, events, dates, names, concepts, formulas, and so on that measure information (Type I learning). However, an instructor may include short-answer questions requiring concise statements of Type II learning.

Taking Short-Answer Tests

Since short-answer tests are basically recall tests, your best strategy is to provide the required information as quickly and clearly as possible. Long explanations are usually unnecessary and a waste of time. One-word responses will usually be judged as equal to a one- or two-sentence response if you can sufficiently answer the question with one word. There are two types of short-answer questions. One form gives you a short space following the question to write a brief response of usually no more than a sentence or two. The other type includes a blank in the body of a sentence, which you are to fill in a single word or two (these are frequently called fill-ins). Examples of each type are given below.

Example of a short-answer question requiring a sentence or two:

Define *Political Socialization.*

If you have followed earlier study suggestions (Chapter 2), you will have developed a good summary statement that can serve as a good definition of *Political Socialization.* The fact that you have defined this term in your own words means that it will be relatively easy to recall.

Another example, from biology:

Briefly diagram a cell undergoing mitosis. Indicate the main stages and what is happening during those stages.

Here you should have already organized your study of cell division around the notion of a "stage-like" process.

Below are two examples of short answers that have blanks to be completed; the first is from psychology.

The term _____ suggests that an individual might show delusions of grandeur or persecution without being schizophrenic.

Another example is drawn from business law:

The _____ is the court order that requires a person to appear in court as a witness.

The following principles should help you with both types of short-answer tests.

Principle 6.13: Write no more than necessary.

Most professors do not like reading long answers or searching for answers while correcting short-answer tests. Short, direct, clearly written responses are best. Consider the following questions and two possible answers.

> Thomas Hardy was a master at using a theme throughout his works. What is the most consistent theme found in the work of Hardy?
> *Answer 1:* Fate
> *Answer 2:* Thomas Hardy included the same theme in most of his works. In a masterful way he blended fate into the themes of seventeenth century England.

Answer 1 is correct, direct, clear, and easily located. Answer 2 is correct, but the specific answer is more difficult to find. In addition, the second answer contains an extraneous error ("seventeenth century"), which occurred due to the length of the response. The more you write, the more opportunities you have to make errors. Professors vary in the length they prefer for a short-answer question. If more detail is preferred, write a long answer. Ask your teacher how long a short answer should be. In general, for a fill-in or sentence completion, write only in the space given. The same is true when a one- or two-sentence response is required. Develop your response so that it fits into the space allotted.

Principle 6.14: With sentence completion or fill-in questions, make your response grammatically correct.

One fairly sure way to miss a sentence completion is to fill in the incorrect form of a word. For example:

An _____ is the most efficient form of transportation.

The answer *train* would clearly be wrong because it is grammatically incorrect. Fill-in questions often provide cues of this sort to the correct response.

> Socrates had been a stonemason and _____.

In this question the answer in the blank must begin with a consonant and not a vowel because of the article *a* used in the question. The answer is *soldier*.

> In the essay, "The Voyage," Irving imagined he saw a _____.

Again the word in the first blank must begin with a consonant. The answer is *fairy kingdom*.

Principle 6.15: Make sure your response makes sense.

Particularly with fill-ins, you should read the item carefully and determine what the blank calls for. For example:

> "The main purpose of a short-answer question is to _____
>
> _____."

Here, the question focuses on the main purpose (the singular form of *purpose* is used), not the two main purposes or secondary purposes; so, the response must describe a single purpose. However, two words are called for, which indicates that the purpose has two words or that a verb form must be included in the response. We know that recall is the main purpose, so we can add a number of verbs to this to make *test recall, assess recall, evaluate recall*—all are correct.

Principle 6.16: If you do not know an answer, then guess.

Guessing is rarely penalized in short-answer tests, so you should always guess. As always, make your guess as informed as possible. For example, consider this question:

> _____ experiments marked the beginning of modern psychology.

Let us say you do not know the answer to this question. There are several reasonable guesses you might make such as *Scientific* or *Well-controlled*. These would be informed guesses because some relevant information was used to generate them. Uninformed guesses may also be good. For example, *Revolutionary* or *Very impressive* would be good guesses because the question relates to the *beginning* of modern psychology. Always try to make guesses that are as relevant as possible. Good guesses may yield extra points and higher grades through partial or full credit.

PREPARING FOR SHORT-ANSWER TESTS

Since short-answer questions are usually only a small portion of an entire test, a lot of specialized preparation is unnecessary. Remember that short-answer tests usually measure recall. And, as we have mentioned, short answers are frequently oriented to facts, concepts, ideas, and so on, which must be stated very succinctly. As you prepare, watch for important ideas, facts, and concepts that could be the subject of short-answer questions. You might also practice some possible short answers to possible questions. As you know from the chapter on essay tests, well-organized answers are always best. Therefore, you should attempt to develop concise, well-organized answers to possible questions about main issues. If you develop good summaries of the material you study, these summaries will be excellent answers to many short-answer questions. As you know, factual information can be remembered by including facts in larger summaries of information. Brief but concentrated practice sessions spaced over three or four days will assist you in remembering facts.

SUMMARY

True-false, matching, and short-answer items appear frequently on tests, yet none of the three is ordinarily used for a whole test. They most often involve questions about facts and information, although each of the three test types may include more complex questions.

To determine whether statements are true or false, you must examine both facts included in the statement and any mentioned relationship between these facts. True-false questions must be read carefully, particularly for absolute and relative qualifiers. Often the correctness of a question will be based on the logical use of these qualifiers. Always answer every true-false item, even if you must guess blindly—you have a 50–50 chance of being correct.

Matching questions require you to match the items in two separate lists. The question list may contain a series of names, dates, or facts that must be matched with the appropriate contributions, events, or results. Begin a matching question with the responses you know, making sure you are following the directions carefully. Systematically work your way through the test until you complete the question. Always guess when you do not know a match.

There are two types of short-answer tests: the fill-in and the type requiring a sentence or two. Unlike true-false and matching, short-answer questions require you to generate an answer. Responses to short-answer questions should contain no more words than necessary and be well organized and logical.

If you use the principles described in the other chapters, you will be able to aggressively attack these three types of tests. The principles for taking each of the three types of test are summarized in the table below.

TAKING TRUE-FALSE, MATCHING, AND SHORT-ANSWER TESTS: SOME KEY REMINDERS

True-False Tests

- Questions including absolute qualifiers, such as *never, always,* and *all,* stand a greater chance of being false.
- Questions including relative qualifiers, such as *most, normally,* and *sometimes,* are most likely to be true.
- Lengthy statements are more likely to be true than short statements.
- If a question has any false parts, the entire item must be false.
- When preparing for true-false tests, use study procedures that facilitate recall of factual information (e.g., acronyms, analogies, loci, and rhymes).

Matching Tests

- First answer the matches you know for sure.
- With longer matching questions, work systematically through the list, marking off items on the answer list as you use them.
- Guessing can be used effectively if you first eliminate several of the matches.

Short-Answer Tests

- Answer the question directly and concisely. Use the space provided as a cue as to how much you need to write.
- Check answers to see that they fit the sentences grammatically and read sensibly.
- Use reconstruction to remember or recall hard-to-remember details.
- If you need to blindly guess, be sure your answer sounds plausible. You could get lucky.

Action Practice

True-False Tests

Developing your ability to take true-false tests involves abilities in three areas: recognizing questions that include only facts and those that are more complex; analyzing questions into component parts in order to establish the correctness of each part; recognizing qualifiers.

A. For the items below, indicate whether you believe each to be a measure of Type I learning (facts), Type II learning (more complex reasoning), or Type III learning (solving problems).

   1. In the respiratory breakdown of glucose, the greatest amount of ATP is formed in the electron transport system.

   2. Isotopes are alternative atoms of the same element.

   3. The second law of thermodynamics states that energy conversions are accompanied by a loss of free energy.

   4. If a red blood cell is placed in a solution and the cell bursts, the solution is hypoosomotic.

   5. Where R = Rydberg constant, c = Velocity of light, and h = Planck's constant, Rhc is equal to the ionization energy of hydrogen.

   6. If the earth did form by accretion of cold particles and planetoids, the internal heat still present today is probably the result of radioactive decay of unstable nuclei.

   7. Galaxy clusters are used as evidence for the Big Bang or Evolving hypothesis for the creation of the universe because explosions do not explode evenly.

   8. Team A serves first in the first game, and Team B wins the game. Therefore, Team A gets to serve first in the second game, since they lost the first game.

   9. A player goes up for a spike and clearly hits the ball on his side of the net, but contacts the net on the follow-through. He will be called for a foul, and the other team will get side-out.

   10. Density, melting point, and boiling point are properties of substances that do not depend on how much of the substance is present or on the substance's shape.

B. For the questions above, analyze each into component parts so that the separate issues in the questions are clear.

C. Review each of the questions and identify all qualifiers.

Answers

Part A

1. This is basically a Type I question measuring facts about the respiratory breakdown of a glucose.

2. This is a Type I question, which is a definition.

3. This is a Type I question, which measures recall.

4. This could be Type I or Type II. If the problem relates to information directly given in class, it would be a recall question. However, if the questions poses a problem not seen previously ("if a red cell is placed in a solution and the cell bursts"), then Type II learning, which involves analysis, may be required to solve the problem.

5. This problem is a Type II learning problem. You must use knowledge about each of the three elements and use that knowledge to determine whether the given formula is correct.

6. This is a Type II problem. You must combine information on several concepts (accretion, planetoids, and decay of unstable nuclei) to determine the accuracy of the statement.

7. This question combines Type I and Type II learning. Type I learning is involved in the factual first part of the question—are galaxy clusters used as evidence for the Big Bang? Type II learning is needed to resolve the *because* clause.

8. This is a Type III learning question. A rule must be applied to a situation in which a correct solution is possible.

9. This is a Type III question. A rule must be applied in a situation in which a correct solution is possible.

10. This may be either Type I or Type II, depending upon whether the content of the question has been seen previously. If the content has been seen previously, it is a Type I question. If it has not, the question is a Type II because it requires some analysis of the properties of substances.

Part B

1. In the respiratory breakdown of glucose, the greatest amount of ATP is formed in the electron transport system. (one part)

2. Isotopes are alternative atoms of the same element. (one part)

3. The second law of thermodynamics states that energy conversions are accompanied by a loss of free energy. (one part)

4. If a red blood cell is placed in a solution and the cell bursts, the solution is hypoosmotic. (one part)

5. Where R = Rhydberg constant, c = velocity of light, and h = Planck's constant, Rhc is equal to the ionization energy of hydrogen. (one part)

6. If the earth did form by accretion of cold particles and planetoids, the internal heat still present today is probably the result of radioactive decay of unstable nuclei. (one part)

7. Galaxy clusters are used as evidence for the Big Bang or Evolving hypothesis for the creation of the universe because explosions do not explode evenly. (two parts)

8. Team *A* serves first in the first game, and Team *B* wins the game. Therefore, Team *A* gets to serve first in the second game, since they lost the first game. (three parts)

9. A player goes up for a spike and clearly hits the ball on his side of the net, but contacts the net on the follow-through. He will be called for a foul, and the other team will get side-out. (two parts)

10. Density, melting point, and boiling point are properties of substances that do not depend on how much of the substance is present or on the substance's shape. (three parts)

Part C

1. Greatest
2. None
3. None
4. None
5. None
6. Probably
7. None
8. None
9. None
10. None

Maximizing Your Test Score

In the previous six chapters we have focused on test-taking behaviors. The goals in these chapters were to help you better understand the purposes of tests, to give you effective strategies for studying and for preparing to take tests, and to give you action principles to use when taking the various types of tests.

There are additional in-class and out-of-class actions you can take to improve your chances of getting good test scores and grades. As shown in table 7.1, some of these actions are directly related to study; others are indirectly related in that they identify you as a serious student.

TABLE 7.1

	Actions Directly Related to Your Studies	Actions that Indirectly Result in Better Scores
In class	Attending to class activities Taking notes Asking questions	Taking part in class activities Developing a positive appearance as a serious student
Out of Class	Reading and studying tests and other reading materials Reviewing notes and other materials Reviewing previous test performance and learning from your mistakes	Making yourself personally known to the professor Working with other students to master course material

In this chapter we will explain the importance of these actions in contributing to better test scores.

IN-CLASS BEHAVIORS

Classes are generally seen by your professors as the most important way they have of helping you learn course material. But they cannot help you unless you take a great deal of responsibility for your own learning. Consequently, the attitude of aggressiveness and self-sufficiency that we have encouraged you to develop in earlier chapters continues as an important theme here. We believe it is extremely important for students to develop an appropriate attitude with regard to time spent in class.

Note Taking

Learning from class activities, particularly lectures, can be rather difficult. Part of the difficulty lies in the fact that information in class comes quickly. If important points are missed, then they are gone without any permanent record, other than what you can remember. Research tells us that without special action on your part, up to 80 percent of class material is forgotten within a few days, and this is for students who stay awake! How does one retain information when the pace of a lecture is fast, when there is no permanent record, and when important points are not repeated? The most frequently used solution is to take notes—to create for yourself a permanent record of class lectures.

Principle 7.1: Prepare yourself for tests by taking good lecture notes.

Many students follow this advice by frantically trying to write everything the professor says. This is not the way to develop a good set of notes. A verbatim record of what the professor says may not be totally useless, but it certainly does not guarantee that you will develop a clear understanding of the material. We suggest the following steps.

Step 1—Find out what is expected of you. At one level, you should find out what goals have been set by the professor for the course. Determine (by asking if necessary) the extent to which class participation is necessary to meet the course goals. Next, determine the general objective(s) of each lecture. Students who have the most information about goals and objectives generally remember more about the material covered and subsequently perform better on tests. This is true in part because they are able to focus more of their learning efforts in the right place. If you do not get advance information about the content and goals of each lecture, then politely ask for this information just before the lecture starts. Most professors will be willing to give a quick overview. You could ask such questions as these: "What will you be discussing today?" "What is the purpose of today's class?"

Step 2—Coordinate your listening and note-taking activities. You

probably already know that it is difficult to listen and take notes at the same time. So, take time to listen! Remember, your goal is to make sense of the material covered. Most professors work very hard to find ways of helping students understand course material. Listen carefully while main points are being explained, and *then* take a break from listening to write down the essential aspects of the explanation you have heard. In most lectures, there will be several natural breaks to give you a chance to write. As far as style is concerned, try to use a simple narrative approach. You do not have to use complex outlines or shorthand writing. Simply try to produce clear readable sentences that will be understandable when you attempt to read them later.

Step 3—Go over your notes as soon after class as possible. Check

your notes for completeness, legibility, and *organization*. Organization is the key to your understanding and remembering course material. It is good practice during note taking to leave extra space on each page to make organizational notes and cues to help you remember the material.

If you find that some of your notes do not fit together in a meaningful way, ask for an explanation during the next class. It may be that the professor will begin the next class by offering comments to help you see the importance of previously discussed details. Try to be alert for these summaries. You do not want to be busy writing details when important explanations occur.

Step 4—Review your notes before taking the test. There appears to

be only a marginal benefit associated with the simple act of writing notes. It is critical that you recognize the importance of reviewing what you have written. Also, when you review your notes, do not simply read them over verbatim, but *restate in your own words* the relevant facts, concepts, and rules you believe will be on the test. If some of the details are hard to remember, try using the memory aids we discussed earlier.

You can increase your ability to benefit from lectures by preparing in advance for each class. The preparation procedures are very similar to those suggested earlier when we gave a detailed account of study techniques. If specific readings are assigned for class sessions, you should at least try to review them before class. Work on the main ideas, rather than reading for detail. You might also find it valuable to review notes from several previous classes. A good time to review previous class notes is right before class begins.

Finally, although research on note taking appears to indicate that each person is likely to find an individual style of note taking, the four step sequence of note taking activities given above should be a part of your style. Beyond this, develop a comfortable and effective style of note taking you can use consistently.

Asking Questions

Asking questions is an important ability that, though requiring little time or effort, many students do not develop. There are at least two benefits of asking questions. One benefit is the increase in your own knowledge about issues or ideas you do not understand. The second benefit is that your questions may give you the kind of exposure that leads to your being identified as a good student. Both of these benefits lead to better test scores.

Principle 7.2: Ask questions to increase your understanding of course material.

Questions should be used primarily to advance your learning. You may recall that we described earlier several different types of learning you may be asked to demonstrate. We have included in Table 7.2 some examples of questions associated with these different types of learning.

TABLE 7.2

Type of Question	Question Characteristics	Examples
Type I: Information	Requests facts Requests a restatement of facts, process	Who wrote . . . ? Can you explain how . . . in another way?
Type II: Manipulating Information	Requests clarification of the elements of a process, concept, or idea	What are the main reasons for . . . ? Is this the sequence of events in a golf swing? Why did England wait so long to confront Hitler?
	Requests ways to organize material to solve a problem or express an idea	What would Picasso's work have looked like if he had expressed himself with words rather than paint?
Type III: Problem Solving	Requests an example of the application of a formula or process	How can the principle of . . . be applied to . . . ?
	Requests the generation of a solution to a problem that has no clear answer	"How can a capitalistic society eliminate poverty?

We do not suggest that class time be turned into question-and-answer sessions. Many of the questions you have will be answered by reading assigned material or will be answered by the professor during class. Make your questions correspond to your note-taking activity. This will increase the probability that your questions are a natural outgrowth of trying to make sense of the material.

Other Class Participation

In addition to asking questions, there are frequently other class-related opportunities to increase your knowledge. Most professors devote a good bit of time to preparing their classes. It is very deflating for them to see students sit in classes looking bored and uninterested and failing to participate in any way. In addition to note taking and asking questions, three ways of improving your image as a serious student are attendance, promptness, and seating.

Attendance. You should attend classes regularly and make sure your teacher recognizes that you are attending. You can do this by saying hello or goodbye or making eye contact upon entering or leaving the class.

Promptness. It is always a good idea to get to class on time and stay until the end of class. It is very disruptive to have students wandering in and out during class. If you find that you must be late on occasion, request permission or inform your teacher that you will be late.

Seating. Scientists who study learning have discovered that students who sit in the front, middle section of a class usually get higher test scores than students sitting elsewhere. The front center location seems to be particularly good for active participation in class.

Principle 7.3: Make your presence in class known by your courtesy, cooperation, and willingness to learn.

The behaviors listed above may sound trivial in and of themselves, but collectively they contribute to the total image of you your professor will develop.

Every grade you receive is a combination of many factors. Performance on tests is a major factor in all grades. But every grade also includes, to some extent, your professor's beliefs about you as a student. If your professor thinks you are rude and shallow, you will be given few breaks. On the other hand, if your professor thinks of you as a serious student and knows your name and face, it is more likely you will be given the benefit of the doubt when needed.

You do not have to be dishonest for your professor to think of you as a good student. However, if you enjoyed a class session or were able to understand because of a good lecture, let your professors know they have helped you. Most students have many good ideas, but because they never discuss them with their teachers, they never get credit for these ideas. You must take responsibility for letting your professors know you, since most professors have too many students to try to get to know everyone. The good students who are recognized by professors have made the effort to make themselves known.

OUT-OF-CLASS BEHAVIORS

A variety of actions taken outside of regularly scheduled classes can lead to improved test scores. Generally, these actions do not involve participation in formally organized classes, but using resources including textbooks, professors, test results, and libraries.

Learning from Textbooks

Principle 7.4: Develop an effective method of studying textbook material.

Besides lectures, textbooks are probably the next most valuable learning resource available to students. As with lectures, your task with textbooks is to find the meaning of material for which you are responsible. However, students invariably find that reading and rereading text materials still leaves them far short of being able to perform well on tests.

To improve your ability to learn text material, first, engage in a series of prereading activities to clarify your goals and give you a look at what you are about to read.

Prereading Activities

1. Read the preface and any introductory chapters designed to give you the overall picture. In most cases, authors will try to tell you in the beginning what they want you to learn.

2. Read chapter outlines and/or skim main headings included in each chapter. Your purpose is to discover how the material is organized. Once you have the main idea, the details can be added to this organized summary.

3. Read any available summaries. It is always helpful to know where you are going before you start. Some authors provide such information in the form of objectives; others provide summary paragraphs.

Once the above activities have been accomplished, reading can be more meaningful. After reading the material, do the following postreading tasks:

Postreading Activities

1. Develop sets of questions that cover the material and conform to expectations set by the professor.

2. Answer your questions, and practice reciting (without notes) these answers.

3. Look for ways to integrate the material into summaries, which can be more easily remembered (review the section on memory if needed).

Some authors suggest complex methods of note taking and underlining to help you with textbook study. We do not think it is absolutely necessary to resort to such elaborate methods. However, you will want to work toward combining your notes from classes with the material learned from texts. In each case, the summaries or notes you do develop should be organized around the questions or issues identified by your professor as being important.

Finding Out More about Course Expectations

We have emphasized in each chapter the value of discovering expectations and knowing grading criteria. In addition to the principles already presented, the following four action principles will assist you in learning your professors' expectations.

Principle 7.5: Know your professors.

Getting to know professors is almost always helpful, since this allows you to learn their beliefs about the course. A small investment of your time can yield large benefits in how you understand the content and express yourself on tests. Because there are usually different points of view on any subject, knowing what the professor believes will give you an advantage. You will have a better chance of providing answers that will be graded highly.

There are many opportunities for acquiring this kind of information. One way is to read something the professor has written on the topic. This will be particularly helpful if your professor is recognized widely as an authority.

Another technique is to make note of points the professor repeats frequently. Most professors stress a few main ideas or concepts. You can use these frequently repeated ideas to organize your own thinking and to prepare for tests.

You may also want to find out what the professor thinks about education. There are several ways to approach teaching. If a professor appears to believe the purpose of education is to separate the best students from the rest, then you should work to be perceived by the professor as one of the best. A good indicator that a professor holds a selective philosophy is the use of curve grading. If, on the other hand, the professor appears to have fairly rigid standards or criteria, you should try to identify these criteria. Ideally criteria will be stated in the course syllabus; however, if criteria are not clear ask for an example of a good test response or what distinguishes a good response from a poor one. In other words, try to find out what the professor is looking for on a test and then plan your study and test preparation around these purposes.

Principle 7.6: Meet with your professors out of class.

There are several reasons for meeting with your professors outside of regular class meetings. Perhaps the most important reason is that these meetings can provide additional opportunities to improve what you know. Of course, you also have the opportunity to display to the professor your sincere interest in the subject. Some of the major reasons for meeting with professors are given below.

You want to make yourself known to your teachers because you want to develop a reputation as a hard working and serious student. This is particularly helpful when tests are graded subjectively, such as essay exams and short-answer tests. Teachers who know you are serious will be more likely to grade your answers as acceptable than if they had no idea of who you are or what you know.

If you are unsure of how to make contact with a professor, see whether office hours are posted. These are times specifically set aside to meet with students. Very few students use these office hours to their advantage, and often students who do use the office hours only do so when they are in trouble due to poor test grades. An aggressive test taker anticipates problems before a test and gets these problems resolved. We recommend that you meet with your teachers early to clear up anything you do not understand about the course material or testing procedures.

Even if an instructor does not post office hours, virtually every professor we have known was willing to make appointments to see students. So, even if you cannot meet your professor during posted office hours or, if no office hours are posted, you can request an appointment. Teachers are interested in helping you learn and will usually do whatever is reasonable to help you learn.

Prepare yourself before meeting with a professor. Identify what you do not understand and prepare some questions, such as those described earlier. Do not be afraid to admit not understanding a point the professor has made, and also indicate that you have thought about the issue. This will show that you are genuinely interested and have at least some understanding of the issues.

Let the professor know you appreciate the help you have been given. Teaching is often a thankless task. Professors derive much satisfaction from hearing that they have helped a student learn. Professors naturally do not want to hear that you think what they teach is useless and irrelevant; find something positive to say, even if that particular course is not your favorite area of study. This is a matter of simple courtesy.

Principle 7.7: Use extra help opportunities.

Two kinds of extra help opportunities are study sessions and additional readings. Although the value of these opportunities varies, being seen at a study or review session cannot hurt. Professors often construct their exams about the same time they hold study sessions and thus sometimes give very strong clues about what will be on a test.

Requesting additional reading can also be quite helpful. When you ask for extra reading, you should give some evidence to your teacher that you have read the material. Read selectively, though. If the suggested reading corresponds closely with the professor's lectures and ideas, you have discovered a valuable resource. Read it carefully. On the other hand, some suggested readings are background material and may not contribute too much to your understanding of course material if you already have a good foundation.

USING TESTS AS LEARNING OPPORTUNITIES

A returned test represents one of the most significant of all opportunities to increase what you know. However, most students totally waste this opportunity by looking only at the test score and discarding the test. A returned test can provide two benefits for you: It can confirm what you thought you knew, and it can identify what you do not know. The following two action principles describe how you can use returned tests as opportunities to improve your understanding and future test scores.

Principle 7.8: Learn from your errors.

Do not throw a test away when you get it back; review the test results carefully. Identify how your answers correspond to, and differ from, your instructor's idea of the correct response. Follow up on the differences, particularly as reflected in your instructor's comments.

Principle 7.9: Look for ways to improve your test scores.

For most issues in science, social science, the humanities, art, and mathematics there are few, if any, absolutely correct answers. As a result, it is always possible to challenge the results of a test. Whether you should challenge a test grade depends on many factors, including how much time you want to devote to preparing a challenge, the probable outcome of the challenge, and the professor involved.

Professors generally recognize that it is possible for them to make errors, even though most professors do correct their tests with great care. Professors want to be both fair and honest in their judgment of your learning. Therefore, if you believe your test has been incorrectly graded, you should prepare your challenge carefully. We do not wish to discourage you from challenging your grade. In fact, we think a challenge of a grade is a useful learning experience. What we want to stress is that you must prepare your challenge so that you demonstrate your understanding and show how much you know, rather than just complain.

A student who complains bases the challenge of a grade on arguments about fairness or relevance of a test. That is, the complaining student uses little or no information and gives little evidence of understanding the course material. For example, complaining students might stress how much hard study and effort was put into the course and how much they felt they learned. Most professors will not be impressed with such arguments and will not consider them to be sufficient evidence to warrant a grade change.

Of course the first thing to look for as you review a returned test paper is an error in the calculation of your test score. Look for errors in addition or subtraction of points in the total grade as well as such errors in individual answers.

When you challenge a grade on grounds other than simple math errors made by the professor, demonstrate your understanding of the material. Develop an argument to justify why you should get a higher grade than you received. Your justification should be solidly based on course goals, facts, and information; it should include carefully constructed, logical arguments.

To prepare a challenge, first review the question, your response, and the professor's reaction. Try to look at the item from the professor's point of view. Second, develop a reasonable argument in favor of your answer. Review the material pertaining to the question and sketch out the ways in which your answer might be considered correct. Third, if you have made some errors, admit to them, but attempt to show that they are relatively minor or do not substantially detract from the overall answer. Finally, do not trust your memory; write out your challenge, and take notes with you when you see your professor.

When you challenge a grade, attend to such specifics as possible variations in interpretation of questions or, perhaps, how the professor misinterpreted your answer. An effective challenge clearly demonstrates that you understand the course material and that this understanding is important to you. In effect, you are saying to the professor, "I know more than this grade indicates." The worst possible result of a well-prepared challenge is that you will know more after the challenge, even if your challenge does not result in a grade change. Most professors will be open to your concerns and will respond favorably.

In some cases a challenge may not be worth the effort; this is a judgment you must make. If you get a very good grade, there is not much point in haggling over a few points that probably will not make much difference. In addition, there are some professors who do not allow students to challenge grades. When this is the case, a challenge will probably not be worth the effort. Use some judgment about the probable success of your efforts and the importance of the issue to you. If you consider the issues important and you want to develop a good challenge, then do it.

CHANGING ANSWERS

It is always a good idea to review your answers before turning in the test paper to make sure you have made no errors. You should check for spelling, grammar, and other mechanical errors and for possible errors in recording answers when answer sheets are used. Many students seem to think that answers should not be changed. However, most studies indicate that changing answers results in higher test scores. No answer should be changed just because you are not sure it is correct. Anytime you are unsure of an answer, carefully consider the alternatives. Try to narrow down the alternatives to as few as you can. Then use your knowledge to consider each alternative. If an alternative other than the one you have chosen looks better to you, the best advice is to change your answer. Most students do change some answers on most tests. These changes usually result in higher test scores.

SUMMARY

The intent of this chapter has been to describe additional action principles to improve your chances of obtaining good test scores. These actions involve your ability to profit from classes and textbooks, your ability to find out exactly what is expected of you, and your ability to convey to your professors that you are a serious student.

It is not enough for you to study hard and try to learn. You must take advantage of the variety of opportunities available to all students to improve your knowledge. Good students are those who use these opportunities wisely and as a result increase their chances of getting good test scores.

Action Practice

The following exercises will help you to prepare for in-class participation.

1. In one or more of your classes, watch some students who are recognized as good students. See if any of their behaviors are similar to the action principles we have presented.

2. Practice making up questions in several subjects. Include at least one or two Type I, Type II, and Type III questions. Ask some of your friends in your classes these questions to see whether they can answer the questions and think that they are good questions.

3. Attend a class or two in which you are not a student (so that you will not have to pay attention to the class content). Carefully watch for class-participation opportunities. Notice questions asked by the teacher and how many students try to respond. Evaluate the quality of the responses. Observe where students are seated and which students participate the most. We think you will be amazed at how many opportunities there are to participate and how few students take advantage of the opportunity. (Very large lecture classes rarely have opportunities to participate unless a lab section is also a part of the course.)

CONCLUSION

You now have the information and action principles you need to develop yourself into an aggressive test taker. This development will take some effort, but your effort should be more than worthwhile. As an aggressive test taker, you will not only learn more, but you will know how to use your knowledge well and get better grades as a result. We would wish you good luck, but we know aggressive test takers do not need luck.

Glossary

absolute qualifier Terms, such as *all, never, always,* that indicate no exceptions to the qualified statement. The presence of an absolute qualifier is more likely to make a statement false than true.

active involvement A necessary part of effective study is to actively involve yourself in the material. You can do this by asking questions, surveying, testing yourself, and so on.

aggressive action Actions taken by students to ensure that they get good test scores. These actions include aggressive preparation for tests, using test-taking principles, and having confidence in one's ability, rather than in luck.

aggressive test taker Students who maximize the potential of their learning by studying effectively, learning the special characteristics of tests, and using their knowledge of the subject and test taking to demonstrate what they know in an effective way.

alternatives The several possible answers that follow the stem in a multiple-choice question.

answer list One of the two lists of items that must be matched with items on a second list (the question list). The answer list is usually the second of the two lists and usually contains names, dates, objects, places.

challenge Aggressively demonstrate knowledge and understanding to counter a lower than deserved test score.

complaint Method used by nonaggressive test takers attempting to improve grades. Complaints are usually characterized by references to effort or emotion.

distractors The incorrect alternatives included in multiple-choice test questions.

essay test   A test requiring construction of a lengthy, well-organized answer to a question.

focused study   Study directed toward learning material that will be on a test.

good question   A question that helps in understanding the material being studied.

grade on the curve   The practice of raising or lowering grades depending on how the whole class performed on a test. Usually about the highest 10 percent of grades will be assigned an *A*, the next 10 to 15 percent will be assigned a *B*, the next 50 to 60 percent will be assigned a *C*, the next 10 to 15 percent a *D*, and the bottom 10 percent an *F*.

grades   The scores received, which indicate the number or proportion of questions answered correctly or incorrectly.

halo effect   The influence of impressions from previous experience upon current ratings. Halo effect may be positive or negative. For example, a good student who normally responds with well-written, thoughtful answers will probably have test responses rated more leniently than a student who appears not to care or to dislike the subject matter.

interest   In order to understand any material, you must be interested in learning the material.

luck   The uncontrollable factor of chance. A test taker who relies on luck will usually receive low scores.

main idea   The important message or the main point of a lecture or written material. Whenever you read or listen, look for the main idea.

memory   The ability to remember information needed to get a good test grade. Memory can be improved by using memory techniques.

multiple-choice question   A test question composed of two parts: The stem presents a question or situation; then several (three to five) alternative answers are provided. The student's task is to select the *one* best answer.

open-book test   A test for which you are allowed to use reference resources.

organization   The sequence of topics and theme employed to write an essay response. The manner in which a response is organized should be clear and effective in demonstrating your knowledge.

organized information summaries   Information reference and indexing guides that are constructed to quickly locate information during open-book tests.

question list   One of two lists of items that must be matched with items on a second list (the answer list). The question list is usually the first of the two lists and rarely contains any questions.

R. D. Bud   A mnemonic device to help you remember the principles for constructing an essay response.

reconstruction   A method of building a memory about information or events by thinking of actions or events associated with what you are trying to remember.

relative qualifier   Such terms as *sometimes, may, usually, on occasion, ordinarily, normally, typically*, which may result in a question being either true or false. The presence of a relative qualifier is more likely to make a statement true than false.

sample   A portion of a larger group or population. A sample is often selected to represent the larger group in order to determine opinions, beliefs, reactions of the larger group without questioning every member of the population. Tests sample knowledge in the same manner. Rather than asking questions about all that was learned, questions are asked about only a portion, or sample, of the knowledge.

stem   That part of a multiple-choice question that presents the question to be answered or the problem to be solved.

study goals   Study purposes that help you focus your study. Study goals may be drawn from books, class notes, and/or study questions.

study skills   Actions you can take to improve your ability to understand what you study.

survey   A brief review of material to be read before actually reading. The purpose of a survey is to prepare you to study.

take-home test   A test you are allowed to respond to outside of class and use available reference resources.

technical language   The language of a discipline. Many disciplines have a vocabulary of terms that describe events, concepts, and so on in that discipline. Proper use of technical language is one way to demonstrate knowledge of a discipline.

test anxiety   The fear of taking tests.

test wise   Awareness of how to take tests. This includes knowing how to use specific features of tests and test formats to get good grades, regardless of the content of the test.

thinking   What most teachers require evidence of on tests. You may demonstrate your ability to think by selecting or constructing a correct response.

types of learning   Information, manipulating information, and problem solving. These represent different expectations teachers might have for tests.

types of questions   Questions oriented to different types of learning: information, manipulating information, problem solving.

work sheet   A helpful aid for developing responses to essay questions. Essentially a blank sheet of paper should be headed with a title or number for each question. All thoughts, ideas, and facts recalled about the question should be noted on this work sheet. When a response is constructed, these notes will save time and effort.

Index

NOTES

NOTES

NOTES

NOTES

NOTES

NOTES

NOTES

NOTES